COVID-19

The Politics of a Pandemic Moral Panic

COVID-19

The Politics of a Pandemic Moral Panic

Barry Cooper, PhD, FRSC
Marco Navarro-Génie, PhD

Acknowledgements

The authors would like to express their deep appreciation for the many people who have helped bring this project to completion. First and foremost, the authors would like to acknowledge and thank the Board of Frontier Centre for Public Policy for entrusting this vital and important research to the authors and providing leadership and vision by supporting this critical public policy research. Without such support and leadership, research and the public dissemination of significant public policy would not be possible. Research and writing about complex public policy issues requires an enormous amount of time, energy, and resources. It is with great appreciation, the authors thank all staff members of Frontier Centre for Public Policy who contributed time and energy into the final manuscript: Gerard Lucyshyn, Deanne Brosnan, and Naomi Lakritz.

The Frontier Centre for Public Policy (FCPP) is an independent Canadian public policy think tank focusing on public policy in Alberta, Saskatchewan, and Manitoba. FCPP research aims to analyze current affairs and public policies and develop effective and meaningful ideas for good governance and reform.

Contents

Introduction

The authors of this paper are political scientists, not medical scientists, immunologists, biologists, or anything similar. We have read many papers in those disciplines and have a reasonable understanding of what they say. We are also of the view that, in any science, distinctions matter, as does the logical coherence of an argument and its connection to the reality of experience. In this respect, as we shall show, many of the scientific reports are not just badly written, and thus difficult to interpret and understand, but often ignore fundamental attributes of scientific discourse — such as a coherent grasp of their own assumptions.

The title of this book, COVID-19 The Politics of a Pandemic Moral Panic, refers in the first instance to a disease, COVID-19. A disease is privative of ease or of comfort, which is not always physical. There are mental as well as spiritual discomforts. There are also social and political discomforts. The term pandemic is here used as an adjective rather than a noun. Whether as an adjective or a noun, pandemic is usually distinguished from epidemic. The etymology is distinct: both contain the Greek term for people (demos). A pandemic includes all (pan) people whereas an epidemic occurs upon or amid (epi) people. This distinction, which is clear enough in Greek, is reflected in the more conventional usage of the World Health Organization (WHO). Epidemics are outbreaks of disease on a smaller (but still quite large) scale than pandemics. Usually, epidemics are confined to countries or regions, whereas pandemics are world-wide or ecumenical, at least in principle.

A pandemic moral panic, again in principle, is an ecumenical moral panic. Our focus is on Canada and occasionally on the United States and other countries, particularly Sweden. We will consider not just the rhetoric of epidemiology but the political consequences of enforcing expert knowledge. In this sense, the book is a case study in power-knowledge, a concept made famous by Michel Foucault, and explained below in section three.

1

Fine. But what is a moral panic? A Google search of 0.36 seconds turns up 44 million references, most of which deal with examples. In fact, the term was introduced by Stanley Cohen in his 1972 book, *Folk Devils and Moral Panics*, which was based on his PhD dissertation in sociology written at the London School of Economics a few years earlier.[1] It is, in short, a relatively recent term in social science. We will use it well in the sense that Cohen did forty-some years ago.[2]

The subject matter of his analysis was the response of British society and its government to fights between two youth subcultures, Mods and Rockers, at Brighton on the south coast of England. The focus of any analysis of moral panic is whether an issue is distorted and exaggerated in such a way as to produce an obvious over-reaction on the part of social and political authorities. This occurred with the Brighton riots. Clearly, riots are a problem and a challenge to social order, but the pragmatic issues involved in such events constitute a separate question from the process that results in a moral panic. That process occurs in several stages: (1) an event or perhaps a person is defined as a threat, perhaps only a vague threat, to existing values, traditions, or interests; (2) the event is simplified and presented in the mass (and now social) media in a stereotypical way; (3) moral barricades are manned by editors, politicians, experts, and other right-thinking people and socially authorized knowers; (4) ways of coping with the disturbance are developed, and eventually; (5) the public profile of the disturbance, event, individual, etc., declines and is forgotten or is retained as a memory and as a diffuse or potential threat; Cohen called this aftermath a "folk devil." The chief emotion associated with a moral panic is fear.

Central to the development of the first four stages of a moral panic are four sets of agents. The most important are the media because they are the source of exaggeration and simplification, prediction of dire consequences if nothing is done, and of the symbolization of both the malign disturbance

---

[1] Stanley Cohen, *Folk Devils and Moral Panics*, 3rd ed., (London: Routledge, 2002). In this paper, we provide citations to sources either in the text or in footnotes. These sources are easily accessible on the internet. Where particularly significant sources are concerned, we provide links.

[2] Pardis Sabeti and Lara Salahi use the term "outbreak culture" in approximately the same way as we use the term "moral panic." See Sabeti and Salahi, *Outbreak Culture: The Ebola Crisis and the Next Epidemic*, (Cambridge: Harvard University Press, 2018).

and the benign agents who will restore order. The second group, whom Cohen called "moral entrepreneurs," is backed by a third, who constitute a culture of social control. This group is comprised of the courts, the police, politicians, and others who are "sensitized" to the "evidence" of disruption and know what to do. Moreover, what they do is justified as a response to a fourth group of agents, symbolized as "public opinion," which in turn has been shaped into a moral panic by the three smaller groups. Cohen went out of his way to stress that there is nothing conspiratorial about this four-fold process. If anything, moral panics are endemic to modern societies and the individuals who fulfil their roles as the process unfolds are simply exemplars of power and authoritative opinion. The pandemic moral panic that has accompanied the outbreak of COVID-19 is merely the latest in a long line of responses to disturbances and "deviance." It is surely not the last.[3]

We may summarize our approach to the COVID-19 outbreak as follows: first, viruses have been part of human life throughout the hominin sequence. Homo erectus got sick from viruses, as did his predecessors and successors. Viruses are older than humanity. Sometimes, viral infections prove fatal; sometimes, the infections recede, and our bodies naturally learn how to deal with them. Today we can measure the movement of viruses across the world, infecting human beings as they travel. We also have the means to discover "novel" viruses and to give them names such as SARS-1 in 2002 or SARS-CoV-2 in 2019. What makes a virus "novel" is not simply a question of science but also of judgment.

It seems self-evident to our common-sense understanding that a severe acute respiratory syndrome is a category that includes both the 2002 and 2019 variants. In this respect, it is akin to the distinct lineages of Neanderthals and Sapiens within the larger category Homo. How close the relationship between the two variants of SARS and the two hominin lineages may be is, of course, a matter of dispute among specialists. With respect to the SARS variants, the specialists all agree that both are beta-coronaviruses similar in some respect to the virus that makes humans suffer from colds and flus.[4] One common-sense expectation is that

---

[3] Mark Honigsbaum, *The Pandemic Century: One Hundred Years of Panic, Hysteria and Hubris.* (New York: Norton, 2019).

[4] "The term coronavirus includes a family of seven known viruses that cause respiratory tract illnesses that range from the common cold to such potentially deadly

humans who develop immunity to seasonal viral infections or even to SARS-1 may be better prepared to resist SARS-CoV-2; that is, the human immune system considers the viruses as least partly identical so that immunity developed to SARS-1 could afford some protection against SARS-CoV-2.[5] John Lee, M.D., summarized the point of this brief excursion into the history of virus spread over the past couple of decades: "The spread of viruses like COVID-19 is not new. What is new is our response."[6] Our concerns in this paper are the political and social responses, responses that were tributary to the medical responses.

Now let us consider its genesis and the constituent elements of this pandemic moral panic.[7]

---

illnesses as severe acute respiratory syndrome (SARS)." Kathy Katella, "Five Things Everyone Should Know about the Coronavirus Outbreak," *Stories at Yale Medicine*, (July 30, 2020).

[5] This is the argument that explained why the gene sequences of the viruses were similar — or rather, because the gene sequences of the 2019 variant were similar to the 2002 sequence they caused similar diseases, which is why they were both called SARS. Moreover, the common-sense expectation that SARS-1 might provide some immunity to SARS-CoV-2 was borne out of Chinese data (if they are reliable) that showed a lower impact of the 2019 variant in areas where the 2002 variant had previously been widespread.

[6] John Lee, "Science Isn't Meant to 'Follow the Science,'" *Spectator USA*, (July 9, 2020).

[7] A more medical treatment of this problem is Peter C. Gøtzsche, "Corona: An Epidemic of Mass Panic," *Deadly Medicines*, (March 21, 2020).

It All Began in China

Timelines associated with the spread of COVID-19 have changed over the past several months and, with new information, may change again in the future. There seems to be widespread agreement in publicly available sources that individuals with odd flu-like illnesses were observed in China as early as August 2019. Nothing was confirmed until a 70-year-old man with Alzheimer's disease was diagnosed in late December 2019 in Wuhan. According to the *Lancet*, which, despite recent irregularities, remains a flagship English-language general medical journal, the symptoms of this first patient presented around December 1.[8] There also seems to be agreement that by late 2019 the "novel" coronavirus had jumped from an animal to a human being; this is called a zoonotic transmission. At this point, narrative agreement breaks down. Some observers said the transmission from an animal, not yet specified, to a human took place in the Huanan Wholesale Seafood Market, also in Wuhan. It was called a "wet" market not simply because it sold slaughtered live seafood that requires water to live. It was also the site of the live slaughter of pangolins, wolf pups, hares, snakes, raccoon dogs, porcupines, badgers, pigs, chickens, and peacocks.[9]

A second narrative began with the infection of the wife of the patient with Alzheimer's who showed symptoms of pneumonia at the end of the first week in December. She was then hospitalized in an isolation ward. She had no known history of exposure to the Wuhan wet market. Some observers then turned their attention to the Wuhan Institute of Virology, some 12 kilometres away from the market. Others looked at the even closer (280 metres) Wuhan Centre for Disease Control and Prevention.

---

[8] C. Huang et al., "Clinical Features of Patients Infected with 2019 Novel Coronavirus in Wuhan, China," *Lancet*, 395 (2020), 497–506. See also Insight Investigation, "Revealed: Seven-Year Coronavirus Trial from Mine Deaths to a Wuhan Lab," *Sunday Times*, (July 4, 2020).

[9] Jane Dalton, "From Coronavirus to Antibiotics: The Ways We Use Animals 'Still Risk Spreading Disease,'" *The Independent,* (March 18, 2020).

The Wuhan virology lab, which happens to have close ties to the National Microbiology Laboratory in Winnipeg,[10] was built by a contractor for the People's Liberation Army and is associated with the Academy of Military Medical Sciences. It was intended to be a top-level security laboratory (as well as a top-secret one) that would be capable of handling safely the deadliest human pathogens. The Chinese certified it as meeting Biosafety Level Four, the highest security rating available, but many scientists outside China viewed this information skeptically. In 2017, an article in *Nature* raised questions about the safety protocols in Chinese microbiology labs, adding historical weight to the possibility that the virus may have escaped from the Institute of Virology into the human population that frequented the market.[11]

In January 2018, the United States sent scientists with diplomatic status to visit the Hunan virology lab. They discovered that SARS-like coronaviruses from bats could interact with the human receptor for SARS coronavirus, which "strongly suggests that SARS-like coronaviruses from bats can be transmitted to humans to cause SARS-like diseases."[12] The Americans also found that the lab personnel did not follow or practice Level Four security protocols but were closer to Level Two.

---

[10] See CTV News, "Public Health Agency Probes Matter at National Microbiology Laboratory," (July 16, 2019); CBC News, "Canadian Scientist Sent Deadly Viruses to Wuhan Lab Months before RCMP Asked to Investigate," (June 14, 2020). Several already deadly pathogens were sent to the Wuhan Institute of Virology from Winnipeg for gain-of-function experiments (discussed below) that were not conducted in Canada because they were considered too dangerous.

[11] David Cyranoski, "Inside China's Pathogen Lab," *Nature*, 542 (February 23, 2017):
399–400.

[12] Insight Investigation, *Sunday Times*, (July 4, 2020). Indeed, as early as 2007, infectious disease specialists had noted "the presence of a large reservoir of SARS-CoV-like viruses in horseshoe bats, together with the culture of eating exotic mammals in southern China, is a time bomb. The possibility of the re-emergence of SARS and other novel viruses from animals or laboratories should not be ignored." Other critics of consuming exotic animals advocated not just shutting down Chinese wet markets but cutting out meat altogether. This act, apparently, would help avoid future pandemics (*National Post*, June 26, 2002). See also Vincent C. C. Cheng, "Severe Acute Respiratory Syndrome Coronavirus as an Agent of Emerging and Reemerging Infection," *Clinical Microbiology Reviews*, 20 (2007), 664; see also Yi Fan et al., "Bat Coronavirus in China," *Viruses*, 11 (2019): 210.

The Institute of Virology was controversial for another reason. Virologist Shi Zhengli was nicknamed the "bat lady" for directing a team that had accumulated an extensive collection of coronaviruses from the bat caves of southern China.[13] She has also conducted experiments on bat viruses "to find out how they might mutate to become more infectious to humans."[14] These experiments are called "gain-of-function" or GoF experiments. As the name implies, they are intended to generate viruses that may be more pathogenic and/or transmissible than wild viruses or even to generate viruses with attributes that do not exist in nature.[15] That such experimentation is controversial is an understatement.[16] For that reason, the United States has banned GoF experiments from time to time and they have not been conducted in the Winnipeg lab. They were reinstated in the U.S. on December 19, 2017 after having been discontinued since October 2014.[17]

Shi provided a different account.[18] For context, two matters should be borne in mind. First, the Wuhan Institute has been studying bats and bat diseases for a quarter-century. At the time, they were concerned with discovering the origins of SARS-1. It turned out that the cross-species infection from bats to humans was discovered relatively early. The Chinese scientists eventually traced the origin of the SARS-1 virus to a cave in Yunnan province, over 1,200 kilometres south of Wuhan. The nearest relative to SARS-CoV-2 is also a coronavirus that the Wuhan lab isolated from a horseshoe bat found in Yunnan in 2013.[19] This virus, then called

---

[13] The technique of acquiring coronaviruses from this reservoir of pathogens reminds one of a joke of Aristophanes (*Clouds*, 141–66): they swabbed the tiny bat anuses and collected samples of bat feces and urine.

[14] Insight Investigation, *Sunday Times*.

[15] See National Academy of Sciences, "Gain-of-Function Research: Background and Alternatives."

[16] See Michael J. Selgelid, "Gain-of-Function Research: Ethical Analysis," *Science and Engineering Ethics*, 22 (2016): 923–64.

[17] Talha Burki, "Ban on Gain-of-Function Studies Ends," *Lancet Infectious Diseases*, (February 2018).

[18] The original report was by P. Zhou et al., "A Pneumonia Outbreak Associated with a New Coronavirus of Probable Bat Origin," *Nature*, 579 (February 3, 2020): 270–73.

[19] As a result of forest-clearing for palm oil plantations, horseshoe bats were driven into closer proximity to humans, thus making the transfer easier, whether it was

RaTG13, shared 96.4 percent of its genome with SARS-CoV-2. The 3.8 percent of genetic difference is equivalent to between 20 and 50 years of natural evolutionary change. But, as we shall see, that is not the whole story. In any event, how a bat in Yunnan led to an infection in Wuhan has yet to be definitively accounted for. The second contextual factor is the adversarial geopolitical relationship between the United States and China. Specifically, Shi said that President Donald Trump "owed us an apology" for suggesting that SARS-CoV-2 escaped from the Wuhan lab.[20]

On July 15, 2020, Shi emailed *Science* with a reply to a series of written questions (a link is available in the *Science* article in the previous footnote). When asked if a bat "in or close to Wuhan" might have infected someone, she said that she favoured the theory that the virus spread through an intermediate host. She did not speculate on what that host might be, but others have mentioned pangolins, which are found in southern China, are also smuggled into China from Southeast Asia, and are sold for food and traditional medicine in the Wuhan wet market.[21] Nor did she indicate whether any zoonotic transmission took place in Wuhan or elsewhere. She did, however, repeat the observation of an Australian expert on virus evolution noted above, that the divergence in genome sequence between SARS-CoV-2 and RaTG13 was between 20 and 50 years of natural evolution.

However, as just noted, that was not the whole story. Both Shi and the American Defense Intelligence Agency (ADIA) said that the SARS-CoV-2 virus was not genetically engineered. The Americans also said that there was "no credible evidence" that the virus was intentionally released as a biological weapon.[22] The Wuhan lab was, however, capable of conducting cut-and-paste genetic engineering experiments and evidently, in 2015, took a piece of SARS-1 virus and replaced it with a piece from a SARS-like bat

---

direct or via an intermediate animal. See Adam Matthews, "Review of Honigsbaum," *The Pandemic Century, Postdigital Science Education,* (July 20, 2010).

[20] Jon Cohen, "Trump 'Owed us an Apology,' Chinese Scientist at the Center of the COVID-19 Origin Theories Speaks Out," *Science,* (July 24, 2020). The "us" involved was the team she leads at the Wuhan Virology Institute.

[21] See T. T. Lam et al., "Identifying SARS-CoV-2-Related Coronaviruses in Malayan Pangolins," *Nature,* 583 (July 9, 2020): 282–5.

[22] ADIA document quoted in Fred Guterl et al., "The Controversial Experiment and Wuhan Lab Suspected of Starting the Coronavirus Pandemic," *Newsweek,* (April 27, 2020).

virus to make it infectious for humans. However, such changes are easily detectable, "like a contemporary addition to an old Victorian house." The Americans' conclusion, that it was not intentionally released is, obviously, speculative: that there was no evidence of such an action is not evidence of the absence of action. That the Chinese denied doing so was entirely to be expected.

There remains yet another problem: about a third of the original cluster of Wuhan cases had no exposure to the wet market, which meant that COVID-19 was already spreading through inter-human contact. Here is where the circumstantial evidence regarding the Wuhan Institute of Virology needs to be considered. First, as part of an international program, partly funded by the United States, the institute had been undertaking GoF research. As noted, such research is controversial, especially when conducted in labs with less than stellar safety records, including those in the U.S.[23]

One explanation involves the technique used in GoF experiments often called "animal passage." In 2010, a Dutch virologist, Ron Fouchier, was working on a flu virus called H5N1. It was mainly transmitted by humans handling infected birds and was often lethal. Fouchier wondered what it would take to change H5N1 into a virus more easily transmissible among humans and conducted his GoF experiment using ferrets, not cell cultures, to mutate H5N1. Ferrets are, with respect to viruses, genetically close enough to humans so that if a mutated H5N1 virus could be transmitted between infected and uninfected ferrets, the same thing would likely be possible between humans. The mutation occurs naturally in the ferret's body: infect the first animal with pure H5N1, wait till it gets sick, and then infect a second one with a nasal swab, then a third, and so on. With each iteration, the genetic content of the virus is slightly changed. After the 10th iteration of the animal passage, Fouchier observed that an infected animal could transmit the virus to another one in an adjoining cage and not through a direct swab. Animal-passage techniques employed in a GoF

---

[23] See Joby Warrick et al., "Chinese Lab Conducted Extensive Research of Deadly Bat Viruses, But There is No Evidence of Accidental Release," *Washington Post*, (April 30, 2020).

experiment, again to state the obvious, can eventually produce a novel and, for that reason alone, a dangerous virus.[24]

Fouchier claimed the GoF experiment was essential to demonstrate causal relations among genes, mutations, and disease. Thus, it was useful for the preparation of future anti-viral medicines. For whatever reason, by 2020 animal-passage GoF experiments had become both widespread and routine; most were conducted in BSL-4 labs, though Fouchier's was rated at BSL-2. According to Colin Carlson, an expert in emerging infectious diseases at Georgetown University, such GoF experiments helped virologists isolate and classify SARS-CoV-2 shortly after it appeared.[25] Others, notably Richard Ebright at Rutgers, disagreed. Granted, animal-passage GoF experiments, like so many other technical activities, have dual uses. In terms of the accumulation of circumstantial evidence of such GoF activity in the Wuhan lab, however, the important thing is that, compared to cut-and-paste genetic engineering, animal passage experiments are much more difficult to detect. To revert to the *Newsweek* image, they are like new Victorian replica additions to an old Victorian house.

Consequently, animal-passage techniques results are often indistinguishable from the evolution of a virus in the wild. A bat-sourced coronavirus passing thorough 10 ferrets would be difficult, to say the least, to distinguish from a naturally evolved one. It's possible that the Wuhan lab never undertook animal-passage GoF experiments, though this seems highly unlikely. More credible is the notion that such experiments were routinely but secretly conducted. Perhaps more interesting is another consideration. Kristian Andersen of Scripps Research published a widely cited account in *Nature Medicine* that argued "that SARS-CoV-2 is not a laboratory construct of purposefully manipulated virus."[26] The authors went on to discuss "two scenarios that can plausibly explain the origin of

---

[24] The problem was thoroughly discussed in Jon Cohen, "Surprising Twist in Debate over Lab-Made H5N1," *Science*, 335 (March 9, 2012): 1155–56; Martin Enserink and Jon Cohen, "One H5N1 Paper Finally Goes to Press: Second Greenlighted," *Science,* 336 (May 4, 2012): 529–30; Tina Hesman Saey, "Second Blocked Flu Paper Released," *Science News*, 182 (July 14, 2012): 8. The GoF research was controversial for an obvious additional reason: potential bioterrorists might use the information for their own purposes.

[25] Colin Carlson, "From PREDICT to Prevention, One Pandemic Later," *Lancet*, (March 30, 2020).

[26] Kristian Andersen et al., "The Proximal Origin of SARS-CoV-2," *Nature Medicine*, (March 17, 2020): 450–55.

SARS-CoV-2." The second, natural selection in humans following a zoonotic transfer, is less significant than natural selection from an animal host prior to a zoonotic transfer.

The authors do admit that "in theory, it is possible that SARS-CoV-2 acquired … mutations … during adaptation to passage in cell culture," but the evidence of SARS-CoV-2-like viruses in pangolins "provided a much stronger and more parsimonious explanation" of how SARS-CoV-2 acquired its new transmissibility features, namely inter-human infection. The authors did not consider the possibility of animal passage in a laboratory. But as Ebright noted in an email to *Newsweek*, mutation in a laboratory using animal-passage GoF techniques is "identical apart from location" and human intervention, from wild "pangolin-passage" scenarios.[27] Ebright thus concluded that Andersen's reasoning was "unsound" because there was no reason to favour wild-pangolin over other laboratory-based animal-passage events.

To summarize: the Wuhan Institute of Virology was in possession of the virus RaTG13, which shared 96.4 percent of its genetic material with SARS-CoV-2. A 3.8 percent genetic divergence may provide a challenge to an animal-passage bridge, but it would be far more likely than a natural evolutionary series of mutations. Second, the denials Shi published in response to questions Cohen raised in *Science* were, as Ebright said, "formulaic, almost robotic, reiterations of statements previously made by Chinese authorities and state media."[28] Accordingly, they should be given the same validity as bestowed upon Chinese authorities and state media.

Indeed, politics as much as science has informed any accounts of the origin of the SARS-CoV-2 virus that cast the slightest doubt on the official Chinese version. On February 6, 2020 two researchers from the South China University of Technology, Xiao Botao and Lei Xiao, published a paper claiming that "the killer virus probably originated from a laboratory in Wuhan."[29] The paper was soon retracted and the authors said their conclusions were "premature." Research within China contrary to the accepted account would, under normal circumstances, quickly disappear.

---

[27] Guterl et al., "The Controversial Experiments."

[28] Cohen, "Trump 'Owes us an Apology.'"

[29] Radio France International, English edition published by ProQuest, "Conspiracy Theories: US-China Clashes Undermine Credibility of Theory that COVID-19 was Man Made," (September 17, 2020).

Whether that happened in the Xiao-Lei case is not known.[30] In April 2020, Luc Antoine Montagnier, who received a Nobel Prize for his discovery of the HIV-AIDS virus in 2008, also argued that SARS-CoV-2 was made in a laboratory because, he said, it was based on the HIV virus being used as a template. He cited the work of Prashant Pradhan and colleagues at the Kusuma School of Biological Sciences in New Delhi.[31] Both Montagnier and Pradhan were dismissed as being "conspiracy theorists," a term that has often been employed against critics of what may be called the orthodox or mainstream narrative. By then, the Andersen et al. study in *Nature Medicine* had appeared and the notion of an engineered origin to SARS-CoV-2 was effectively debunked though hardly disproved.

In mid-September, however, the controversy reappeared when the *New York Post* reported that a Chinese virologist, Li-Meng Yan, had published a report showing that SARS-CoV-2 displayed "biological characteristics that are inconsistent with a naturally occurring zoonotic virus."[32] Li-Meng had worked at the Hong Kong School of Public Health, which is associated with both the WHO and the PRC, until April 2020. She said she fled because she feared for her safety and implied her fear was connected to work, she had done in December 2019 in human-to-human transmission of the virus. The Hong Kong School of Public Health denied her claim to have conducted research on human-to-human transmission. In addition, they wiped her work from Chinese databases. Whatever one makes of Li-Meng's biography, the argument she made in *Unusual Features of the SARS-CoV-2 Genome* would have attracted the disapprobation of Chinese officials.

The two arguments that gave greatest support to the orthodox narrative were the Andersen et al. "natural origin" article in *Nature Medicine* and what might be called the "pangolin theory." She cited several critics of the

---

[30] Jay Hilotin, "COVID-19's Origins Shrouded in Mystery: Here's Why," *Gulf News: Dubai*, (April 29, 2020).

[31] Pradhan et al., "Uncanny Similarity of Unique Inserts in the 2019-nCoV Spike Protein to HIV-1 gp120," *bioRXxiv*, (preprint), (January 31, 2020).

[32] Tamar Lapin, "Chinese Virologist Posts Report Claiming COVID-19 was made in Wuhan Lab," *New York Post*, (September 14, 2020); see also Li-Meng Yan et al., *Unusual Features of the SARS-CoV-2 Genome Suggesting Sophisticated Laboratory Modification Rather than Natural Evolution and Delineation of Its Probable Synthetic Route*, (New York: Rule of Law Society and Rule of Law Foundation, n.d.). The Rule of Law Society and Foundation are supported by Guo Wengui, a wealthy Chinese critic of Beijing.

Andersen et al. theory and pointed out that at least two members of his team had been connected to, or honoured by, China. As noted above, the "natural origin" theory relied on the existence of RaTG13, which shared 96.4 percent of its nucleotide sequence with SARS-CoV-2. She queried whether RaTG13 actually existed in nature and whether its genetic sequence was truthfully reported. "Therefore the theory that fabricated scientific data has been published to mislead the world's efforts in tracing the origin of SARS-CoV-2 has become substantially convincing and it interlocked with the notion of SARS-CoV-2 is of a non-natural origin." That was the double-edged hypothesis she defended by arguing that the genomic features of SARS-CoV-2 indicated "that the virus is a product of laboratory modification beyond what could be afforded by simple serial viral passage" using animals. In particular, she argued that a specific site on the SARS-CoV-2 spike protein had been fabricated as the result of genetic manipulation, and speculated that "the purpose of this manipulation could have been to assess any potential enhancement of the infectivity and pathogenicity of the laboratory-made coronavirus."

She also criticized the "pangolin theory" citing recent studies published in *Nature* and other credible sources that indicated flaws in the earlier published data. The evidence and data in support of the "pangolin theory," she said, "are largely suspicious and likely fraudulent. Those fabrications would serve no purpose other than to deceive the scientific community and the general public so that the true identity of SARS-CoV-2 is hidden." Li-Meng's contention was plain: "SARS-CoV-2 is a laboratory-enhanced virus and product of gain-of-function research." It could have been created both easily "using available materials and well-documented techniques" and relatively quickly, in about six months. Her concluding recommendation was expected: "The possibility that the SARS-CoV-2 virus could have been created through gain-of-function manipulations at the WIV [Wuhan Institute of Virology] is significant and should be investigated thoroughly and independently."

As a postscript to the Li-Meng story, we may note two things. First, within a week, her Twitter account was suspended because the social media company said she had violated "Twitter rules" by publicizing her own work. Second, the *Lancet* COVID-19 commission stated, along with a number of ex cathedra remarks on political and social issues, that "research into the origins of SARS-CoV-2 should proceed expeditiously, scientifically, and objectively, unhindered by geopolitical agendas and misinformation." On the surface, such research would agree with Li-Meng's recommendation. However, the *Lancet* authors did not mention China and yet they managed to anticipate "open scientific collaboration" regarding "the possibility of laboratory involvement in the origins of the pandemic." It is clear, however, that they considered a laboratory origin to be unlikely, citing Andersen et al. as providing evidence of a naturally occurring virus and dismissing "baseless conspiracy theories" and unnamed allegations without naming any.[33]

If the circumstantial case (including Li-Meng's argument) in favour of the origin of SARS-CoV-2 in the Wuhan Institute of Virology is persuasive, the next element in the puzzle seemed comparatively straightforward. Even the most mechanically safe and effective laboratory with the most well-trained staff (and the Wuhan facility exhibited neither of these attributes) is susceptible to human error. A lab worker might accidentally contract a virus, fall ill, go home, and pass it on to a family member who goes shopping at the Huanan market. Both foregoing narratives and common sense indicate that accidents happen when human beings undertake risky actions. The Chinese are not exempt. Nor are they exempt from responsibility for the consequences of their actions. That is, whether one accepts the story that the virus evolved through natural selection and first entered the human population from the wet market or that it leaked from the Wuhan Institute of Virology, it is also clear that Chinese authorities were anything but forthcoming in making public what they knew.

Circumstantial evidence regarding the possibility of a leak from the Wuhan lab does not constitute proof and so provides the Chinese with the expected cover of deniability. Whether it is plausible or not is a political question, not a matter of epidemiology. This is why Shi's supporters and the official statements of PRC authorities declare, often in the face of contrary evidence, that "the Wuhan facility was state-of-the-art and presumably operating with a high degree of care." The authors of that statement then called for "a strong surveillance program" that necessarily "will require goodwill and co-operation with other countries and the

---

[33] *Lancet* "COVID-19 Commission Statement on the Occasion of the 75th Session of the UN General Assembly," (September 14, 2020): 1, 4.

WHO."[34] The authors do not say how confident they are that either China or the U.S. would cooperate in such a program. David Cyranoski, writing in *Nature* (June 5, 2020) simply declared the majority opinion, that bats passed on the virus to an intermediate animal, which then passed it on to humans. He said nothing of the trustworthiness of the Chinese, but criticized the "unsubstantial theories," promoted by President Donald Trump, of a laboratory leak. The fact that the Wuhan Institute of Virology was located in the same city where the outbreak first took place "is probably just a coincidence."[35] Such a contingency, like the conclusions of Imperiale and Casadevall, had nothing to do with biological expertise. They reflect Cyranoski's political judgment.

Moreover, when we consider PRC officials' subsequent behaviour, such political judgments look increasingly dubious. We noted above that there was general agreement on the timelines of the outbreak. The first patient was identified no later than December 1, 2019 and his wife a few days later. The obvious implication was that by the second week of December 2019, physicians in Wuhan knew of at least one case where the virus likely spread from one human to another. By the third week in December, doctors in Wuhan had observed a "cluster of pneumonia cases with an unknown cause." By Christmas, two medical staff were suspected of having contracted viral pneumonia and were quarantined (*New York Times*, February 7, 2020). On December 30, Dr. Li Wenliang, an ophthalmologist, informed a group of other doctors in Wuhan about an outbreak of an illness resembling SARS and urged them to take protective measures. One may conclude with confidence that the evidence for human-to-human transmission was growing.[36]

---

[34] Michael J. Imperiale and Arturo Casadevall, "Rethinking Gain-of-Function Experiments in the Context of the COVID-19 Pandemic," *American Society for Microbiology Journal*, 11 (August 2020), emphasis added.

[35] See also Jamie Metzl, "Origins of SARS-CoV-2" *Newsletter*, (April 16, 2020).

[36] There is now established evidence that transmission of the virus had made its way to Europe by late December 2019. See Mary Van Beusekom, "Study: COVID-19 Detected in France in Late December," Centre for Infectious Disease Research and Policy (CIDRAP, University of Minnesota), (May 5, 2020), https://www.cidrap.umn.edu/news-perspective/2020/05/study-covid-19-detected-france-late-december.

The next day, the Wuhan Municipal Health Commission announced that it had "not found any obvious human-to-human transmission and medical staff infection." Front-line doctors in Wuhan thought otherwise and two were suspected of having contracted the virus. On New Year's Day, the Wuhan Public Security Bureau (PSB) picked up Li and accused him of spreading rumours. As is customary among guests of the PSB, Li acknowledged his errors and promised not to commit any additional "unlawful acts." Seven others were also arrested but knowledge of what happened to them in PSB custody is held only by the PSB. One should nevertheless note the obvious: the PSB is not an organization with expertise in public health. It tells the various health commissions what to say and what to do, not vice versa. However, one characterizes the People's Republic of China, it is a regime where police agencies such as the PSB play a leading role.

That same New Year's Day, the Hubei Provincial Health Commission, which included the City of Wuhan, ordered a genomics company that had tested several samples of the virus to destroy any remaining samples and cease testing. They were also told to stop providing results of their tests to Wuhan hospitals. According to the *New York Times* (January 4, 2020), 175,000 persons left Wuhan that day.

Meanwhile, in Wuhan, evidence of human-to-human transmission increased, but on January 3 the National Health Commission of China ordered labs not to publish any further information related to the new disease and to destroy or surrender to the commission any remaining samples of the virus in their possession. The Wuhan Municipal Health Commission issued a statement that "preliminary investigations have shown no clear evidence of human-to-human transmission and no medical staff infections." This statement was repeated on January 5 and reiterated next day in the *New York Times*, along with the advice of Dr. Wang Lingfa, an expert on emerging diseases at an institute run jointly by Duke University and the National University of Singapore, that "we should not go into panic mode." That same day, the U.S. Centers for Disease Control in Atlanta offered to send a team to assist Chinese medical scientists, but their offer was rebuffed.

On January 8, the WHO issued a statement that reiterated a remark made a week earlier that several cases of pneumonia had been diagnosed in Wuhan from an unknown cause. The WHO then praised China for having so quickly diagnosed and managed the outbreak: "WHO does not recommend any specific measures for travelers. WHO advises against the application of any travel or trade restriction on China based on the information currently available." On January 10, the *New York Times* again quoted the Wuhan City Health Commission that "there is no evidence the virus can spread among humans." That same day, Li began coughing and developed a fever after having unknowingly treated a patient with the virus a few days before. He was hospitalized on January 12 and died three weeks later.

About the same time, a Toronto software company called Blue Dot (after Carl Sagan's description of an image of the Earth taken from Voyager One as a "pale blue dot"), used a combination of artificial intelligence plus a capacity to scan thousands of news articles in 65 languages. On New Year's Day, Blue Dot informed its clients — one of which was the government of Canada — that a new and unidentified illness had appeared in Wuhan. Two weeks later, they published a paper integrating these health data with airline flight data to predict where the virus was likely to show up next.[37] It seems to us that if a commercial operation such as Blue Dot could accurately detect the initial outbreak and accurately predict its spread, then government intelligence agencies, particularly in the United States, would have at least the same capability.

Apparently, the Chinese authorities thought differently. The Wuhan City Health Commission continued to report in early January that no medical staff had been infected and "no clear evidence of human-to-human transmission had been found." No clear evidence, one may infer, was not as big a lie as previous statements about no evidence. On January 14, five weeks after the evidence of human-to-human transmission first appeared in Wuhan, the WHO repeated the Wuhan City Health Commission "finding." That same day, the Canadian Public Health Agency said the risk in Canada was "low." As Blue Dot predicted, coronavirus cases had by then been diagnosed in Thailand and Japan, which may have inspired the Wuhan Municipal Health Commission to acknowledge, on January 15, that "the possibility of limited human-to-human transmission cannot be ruled out." On January 17, the Americans

---

[37] Isaac Bogoch et al., "Pneumonia of Unknown Aetiology in Wuhan China: Potential for International Spread via Commercial Air Travel," *Journal of Travel Medicine*, (January 14, 2020); Eric Niiler, "An AI Epidemiologist sent the First Warnings of the Wuhan Virus," *Wired*, (January 25, 2020); see also *U of T News*, (March 27, 2020).

announced that travelers from Wuhan would have to undergo screening for symptoms associated with COVID-19. Three days later, Theresa Tam, Canada's chief public health officer, said that "out of an abundance of precaution" travelers from "virus-infected areas would be asked to report any flu-like symptoms." On January 23, the first Canadian patient with COVID-19 was admitted to Sunnybrook Hospital's emergency department in Toronto. A week later, Tina Namiesnikowski, president of the Public Health Agency of Canada, told a parliamentary health committee that "the system is working as expected."[38] Tam reiterated that voluntary self-isolation for symptomatic travelers was all that was needed in Canada and "there is no evidence" that it is necessary to quarantine asymptomatic persons arriving from "virus-infected areas." She did not mention China.

A couple more January events might be noted. On January 22, the director-general of the WHO, Tedros Adhanom Ghebreyesus, again praised the way China had dealt with the outbreak. By then, millions of persons had left Wuhan, travelling around China for the Lunar New Year celebrations and travelling abroad as well. An unknown, but presumably significant, number of them were carrying the virus.[39] Next day, Chinese authorities began a quarantine lockdown of Wuhan. On January 30, the WHO declared the COVID-19 outbreak a "public health emergency of international concern." Six weeks later, the WHO declared that the outbreak constituted a pandemic.

Most Canadians, who may or may not be ethnically Chinese, have never visited China. They may have favourable or unfavourable views of the PRC, just as they may have favourable or unfavourable views of the WHO, but it is unlikely that they have ever had any direct experience of either. China may no longer exemplify the cliché of the mysterious East, but for most Canadians the image of that country is mediated by socially authorized knowers and their specialized knowledge.

As is clear from the chronology of the COVID-19 outbreak in Wuhan, former president George W. Bush was clearly wrong when he said that China would become a "responsible stakeholder" when in 2001 it joined

---

[38] When she resigned in September 2020, Namiesnikowski noted that she and Tam made "an exceptional team."

[39] Shadi Hamid, "China is Avoiding Blame by Trolling the World," *Atlantic*, (March 19, 2020).

the World Trade Organization (WTO).[40] From December 2019 and possibly earlier, PRC officials knew what was happening in Wuhan; namely, that a contagious virus was at large. Whether it came from a wet market or a more sinister source was secondary. Chinese authorities "chose to cover up, obfuscate and suppress the truth about COVID-19." Indeed, "China lied in an aggressive, systematic and pervasive fashion." According to Burton and Byers, China lied to the WHO as well as to the rest of the world.[41] Assuming that members of the WHO were unaware they were being lied to, China breached articles Six and Seven of the WHO International Health Regulations, which it was legally obliged to uphold.[42]

There was one obvious exception to the general credulity among the nations of the world to accept the PRC's and WHO's assurances on the absence of early awareness of human-to-human transmission of COVID-19: Taiwan. As early as mid-December, Taiwan both reported to the WHO that COVID-19 was humanly contagious and acted on the intelligence that was available from Wuhan. Taiwanese authorities knew from experience that PRC statements were not to be trusted. Moreover, having been excluded from the WHO at China's behest, they also distrusted WHO statements because they viewed that organization as a front for the PRC. Accordingly, during the early weeks of the outbreak, when the rest of the world was listening to and accepting underestimated threats issued by the WHO, Taiwan was compelled to make its own estimates and to act on them, In short, Taiwanese self-reliance, a consequence of the PRC/WHO policies, served them well. By March 2020, the rest of the world had noticed that Taiwan was dealing quite well with the outbreak, which was exactly what Beijing did not want. And so, began Beijing's disinformation

---

[40] See the remarks of Sen. Marco Rubio, "Coronavirus: More Proof China is Unfit for Global Role," *Real Clear Politics*, (February 19, 2020); Marcus Kolga, "When Will the Chinese Government be Held Accountable for the Coronavirus?" *Maclean's*, (March 17, 2020); Sarah Teich, *Not Immune: Exploring Liability of Authoritarian Regimes for the COVID-19 Pandemic and its Cover-Up*, (Ottawa: Canadian Security Research Group and Macdonald-Laurier Institute, 2020): 69–74.
[41] Charles Burton and Brett Byers, "Holding China Accountable for the COVID-19 Cover-up," *Inside Policy*, (June 2020): 24.
[42] For a comprehensive account of China flouting its legal obligations, see Teich, *Not Immune*. In late May 2020, Donald Trump announced the U.S. was terminating its relationship with the WHO, saying that the organization had become a puppet of China. See *Medscape*, (May 29, 2020).

campaign against Taiwan and its own narrative rewrite to portray the PRC in a more favourable light.[43]

There is not much doubt that Taiwan was correct in its suspicion of Beijing's underreporting on Wuhan. Were they also right about the WHO? It is certainly true that the WHO did nothing to disseminate the lessons learned from Taiwan's response to the COVID-19 outbreak. It is also clear that the reason the WHO said nothing about Taiwan's relative success is that the PRC forbade any acknowledgment of it. Those who counter that the WHO's silence regarding Taiwan's success was a condition for PRC cooperation, are burdened with the necessity of citing instances when Beijing was helpful. This they have been unable to do, which leads to the obvious conclusion: "From the outset of COVID-19's outbreak, the WHO's obligation to prepare the world was subordinated to its leadership's determination to protect China from scrutiny. Informants who rang the alarm were disregarded and information that could have averted a calamity was withheld from the world."[44]

Charles Burton drew the most important implication: "So, the question looms: did politically motivated misinformation, issued by Beijing, and uncritically related to the world via the WHO, lead to massive numbers of unnecessary deaths and economic hardship around the world?"[45] Another

---

[43] J. Michael Cole, "How Taiwan is Leading by Example: The Global War on the COVID-19 Pandemic," Macdonald-Laurier Institute, Commentary, March 2020; see also Kurt M. Campbell and Rush Doshi, "The Coronavirus Could Reshape Global Order," *Foreign Affairs*, (March 16, 2020); see also Kathy Gilsinan, "How China is Planning to Win Back the World," *Atlantic*, (May 28, 2020).
[44] Kapil Komireddi, "COVID-19's Willing Accomplice," *The Critic*, (April 23, 2020).
[45] Charles Burton, "Beijing's Coronavirus Bungling Makes Canada's Choice on Huawei even Easier," *Globe and Mail*, (April 24, 2020); see also Amy Karam, "Will COVID-19 Shift Huawei 5G Debate to Economic Security and Global Competitiveness?" Canadian Global Affairs Institute, Policy Perspectives, (June 2020). A study from the University of Southampton estimated that reductions of up to 95 percent in the spread of COVID-19 (and concomitant reductions in "unnecessary deaths and economic hardship") were possible if PRC authorities had intervened in the Wuhan outbreak three weeks before they did. That is, during the early period when the existence and infectious nature of the virus was known to authorities but suppressed. See Shengjie Lai, et al., "Effect of Non-Pharmaceutical Interventions for Containing the COVID-19 Outbreak in China," *MedRXiv*, (March 13, 2020). For a detailed, but in our view rather naïve account of the WHO response,

question looms as well, which Professor Burton likely thought of and Western intelligence agencies are even more likely to have investigated: Was the PRC's under-reporting and systematic lying followed by extensive travel out of, but not into, Wuhan, a deliberate act to spread rather than contain the virus?

Our major point is pretty clear: however, the COVID-19 pandemic began, it began in China.[46] And China, for most Canadians, is a somewhat enigmatic locale even if it is not seen as a threat. The Chinese origin of the pandemic is significant, however, because of the increase in Chinese importance and power over the past generation. So far as the present discussion is concerned, it is somewhat surprising that China's role in the genesis of the COVID-19 pandemic has played almost no part in the accompanying moral panic. This may have been because the director-general of the WHO, Tedros, admonished the world early on that imposing travel restrictions on China would be "discriminatory." Indeed, such restrictions would be discriminatory; that was the whole point of them. But for Tedros, this was meant to suggest racism. Downplaying Chinese responsibility may also have been a result of the behaviour of WHO officials such as Bruce Aylward, the team leader of the joint mission between the WHO and the PRC — and a Canadian — who refused even to utter the toxic word "Taiwan" when a Hong Kong reporter asked him directly about the island nation's obvious success. A few weeks later, Aylward refused, without explanation, to leave his safe perch in Geneva and appear before a parliamentary committee in Ottawa to discuss the

---

see Gabriel Blouin-Genest et al., "WHO Global Response of COVID-19: Communicating Risk/Risky Communications, Rapid Results Report, Phase 1: December 31, 2019 to January 31, 2020," (University of Ottawa, Université de Sherbrooke, Centre on Governance, Working Paper Series, Research Paper No. 01/20/EN, May 2020).

[46] The first epicentre or "hotspot" outside China was in Iran, specifically the "Holy City" of Qom. According to the *Wall Street Journal* (March 11, 2020), Qom is also the site of Iran's main economic links to China. From Iran the virus apparently spread to Canada, New Zealand, and New York City. See Negar Mojtahedi's report, Global News, (March 1, 2020) and Noam Blum, *Tablet*, (March 13, 2020); see also Teich, *Not Immune*, 75–8, and Maysam Behravesh, "The Untold Story of How Iran Botched the Coronavirus Pandemic," *Foreign Policy*, (March 4, 2020).

links between China and the WHO.[47] Tam, who had spent much of her career at the WHO — and still sits on important WHO committees, and like Tedros, is a graduate of the University of Nottingham — has never emphasized the origin of the virus or the appalling behaviour of Chinese officials. Also, like Tedros, starting with a press conference on January 29, she equated criticism — or even mention — of the PRC with racism. When asked for details of racist attitudes, she could provide no examples. This is hardly surprising since many of the critics were members of the Chinese Canadian communities in Vancouver and Toronto. She was also entirely oblivious of the fact that by offering a commentary on racism she was making a political and not a medical or epidemiological observation, her supposed specialty and bureaucratic remit.

As for the government of Canada, led by a person whose admiration of the PRC has been extensively documented over the years,[48] the April 2 press conference by Health Minister Patty Hajdu was particularly revealing. Before assuming responsibility for Canadians' health, Hajdu was a graphic designer; the prime minister picked her as the post-election replacement for Jane Philpott, M.D., who had been purged before the 2019 election from the Liberal caucus for holding incorrect opinions on the SNC-Lavalin scandal and for supporting then-attorney general Jody Wilson-Raybould on the question of the rule of law. At the press conference, Hajdu berated a CTV reporter for "feeding into conspiracy theories" by daring to question whether Chinese data were reliable. Or rather, the reporter asked for a Canadian response to observations by American intelligence officials that the Chinese statistics were worthless. Hajdu immediately added the cliché invocation that "we're all in this together."[49] So long as COVID-19 exists anywhere, "it exists in all our countries." Accordingly, "we actually have to work together as a globe." More specifically, Hajdu said "there is no indication that the data that came out

<hr>

[47] Steven Chase, "WHO Balks at Ottawa's Request that Key Adviser Testify before MPs," *Globe and Mail*, (April 29, 2020); See also *True North Wire*, (April 30, 2020); (August 19, 2020).

[48] For a recent account, see Ezra Levant, "China Virus," Rebel Media (2020); see also Raymond de Souza, "Not the Usual Diplomatic Prattle," *National Post*, (June 26, 2020).

[49] Steven Chase, *Globe and Mail*, (April 2, 2020). In this context, see the remarks of Terence Corcoran, "Surviving the CLICHÉ-19 Pandemic," *Financial Post*, (May 12, 2020).

of China in terms of their infection rate and their death rate was falsified in any way." Not even the Chinese believed that: within two weeks the PRC doubled the estimated number of deaths in Wuhan.[50] For most Western analysts, the revised Chinese number was still a gross under-estimation.

Despite the best efforts of the WHO and their Canadian followers in government, the malign reality is that China's role in the COVID-19 pandemic remains stubbornly relevant. China is rather like a miasmic mist that renders the other constituent elements of the COVID-19 moral panic obscure.

---

[50] According to the *New York Times* (August 19, 2020), American intelligence agencies believe that Chinese officials in Wuhan hid the initial outbreak from the central leadership in Beijing for several weeks in January. Whether the orders to hide the information about the Wuhan epidemic originated in Beijing or elsewhere seems to us to be a secondary detail: Chinese officials were responsible. The next day, Maria van Kerkhove, head of the WHO's emerging diseases unit, still maintained it was "rare that an asymptomatic person actually transmits onward to a secondary individual."

Moral Entrepreneurs

From late January until mid-March, Canadian public health officials minimized the risks of COVID-19. Tam told members of the parliamentary health committee on January 30 that infection by asymptomatic carriers of the virus was "rare and very unlikely." On February 5, she told the committee that Chinese case reports had not been verified. Vancouver East NDP MP Jenny Kwan asked her if Canada had contacted the Chinese officials directly. Tam replied that determining asymptomatic transmission is "quite a difficult piece of epidemiology." She added that when persons are showing symptoms, such as vigorously coughing, "that, we believe, [is when] this virus is transmitted." To state the obvious: Tam's response did not address Kwan's question. Even more curious, if asymptomatic carriers were not a problem, it would have been preferable on common-sense grounds alone to quarantine only those with symptoms, not everyone. The basic justification for the lockdown, in other words, had very weak medical support. The implications of the relative threat of asymptomatic carriers were not discussed for another dozen weeks.[51] There is, in any event, something quite bizarre about the notion of asymptomatic or, as they were sometimes called, "silent" carriers. These were persons, to repeat, who were sick but presented no symptoms. On common-sense grounds, if such a possibility were widely accepted, health-insurance companies would have a big problem, students could claim to be sick and skip school, and ordinary workers could do the same thing and skip work. Who needs such inconveniences as symptoms to declare yourself sick? The point is not that there were no asymptomatic carriers — some models suggested between 30 and 60 percent of transmission

---

[51] See Cassidy Morrison and Madison Dibble, "WHO Walks Back Statement that Asymptomatic Coronavirus Spread is 'Very Rare,'" *Washington Examiner*, (June 9, 2020). By then, the WHO had drawn a super-fine distinction between asymptomatic carriers and pre-symptomatic carriers. Of course, before the symptoms presented, the two kinds of carriers' conditions were utterly indistinguishable.

takes place that way (*New York Times*, June 27, 2020). The point, rather, is that health officials did not want to discuss such ambiguities as the different robustness of individual immune systems or why some individuals who contracted COVID-19 showed no symptoms. It was preferable to present a clear and simple picture.

Meanwhile, Canada kept its borders open to the world. The only measures Canada Border Services took were to post information on arrival screens at airports in Vancouver, Montreal, and Toronto, and hand out pamphlets. Tam several times reiterated the unlikelihood of asymptomatic transmission and recommended travelers from Hubei stay at home for two weeks. Hajdu repeated her remarks on the declining importance of borders. "A virus knows no bounds," she said on March 6. The implication, carried out by Canada Border Services, was that screening foreigners and returning Canadians was futile. That same day, Tam allowed that borders are, in fact, useful because they are convenient places to "provide people with information" about what to do when they get sick.

On February 9, Global Affairs Canada announced that Canada was shipping about 16 tonnes of personal protective equipment to China. Minister of International Development Karina Gould remarked that Canada was "saddened" by the impact of COVID-19, "especially the loss of life in the Chinese population." The prime minister, during an effort to gain support from African countries for a temporary seat on the UN Security Council, stated from Ethiopia that "we are confident that in Canada the risk remains low." That was why he was willing to respond quickly to "the Chinese request for medical equipment." Both in terms of domestic and foreign policy, until early March Canada saw no substantive threat from COVID-19.

Then, around mid-March, everything changed. On March 11, the WHO declared COVID-19 to be a global pandemic. Five days later, on March 16, Neil M. Ferguson and his team released a badly written "Report 9: Impact of Non-pharmaceutical Interventions (NPIs) to Reduce COVID-19 Mortality and Healthcare Demand."[52] Before examining the impact of the Ferguson document, let us consider another social science term: power-knowledge.

The concept *pouvoir-savoir* was developed by Michel Foucault to refer to power that is not so much an instrument of coercion as a diffuse reality

---

[52] Imperial College COVID-19 Response Team, (March 16, 2020).

"embodied" in discourses. By Foucault's argument,[53] power is not possessed or wielded by people or groups through acts of domination but, he argued, is enacted throughout society as a kind of regime. Foucault called this phenomenon a "regime of truth" that by implication, is in flux or is constantly "negotiated" among major and sometimes minor actors. "Power-knowledge" signified that power is constituted through accepted forms of knowledge. Today, the chief form of knowledge is found in a scientific understanding that is instantiated in specific institutions whose personnel have the status of truth-tellers.

Within the context of any particular regime of truth, the "battle" for truth is conducted in terms of the rules by which the true and the false are separated and power is linked and connected to the true. That is, truth is not something discovered but, for Foucault, is a reality that is at least in part produced by power. We need not go into details regarding the metaphysics of Foucault's concept or the problem of relativism and historicism to understand that power-knowledge is a major source of contemporary social discipline and political conformity. From the eighteenth century on, for example, the discipline embodied in a mental asylum has been connected to the discourse of psychiatry, the surveillance of the police, and the civilian bureaucracy to the discourse of administrative order. This concept of power-knowledge, it seems to us, provides a helpful theoretical context by which the Ferguson document was translated both into a pervasive public policy and into resistance to the consequences of that policy.

Ferguson's team's report reproduced the output of a computer model that compared the expected number of deaths in the U.S. and the U.K. with or without various "non-pharmaceutical interventions." Again, to state the obvious, non-pharmaceutical interventions, absent an anti-COVID-19 vaccine, were the only interventions available.[54] At that time, the British government was prepared to push the herd-immunity approach that would allow persons in non-vulnerable categories to catch the virus, develop immunity to it, and, when a large enough portion of the

---

[53] For details, see Barry Cooper, *Michel Foucault: An Introduction to the Study of His Thought* (Toronto: Edwin Mellen Press, 1981) or Clarissa R. Hayward, "De-Facing Power," *Polity* 31 (1998): 1–22.

[54] Mayo Clinic, "There are two paths to herd immunity for COVID-19 — vaccines and infection." *Herd Immunity and COVID-19 (Coronavirus): What You Need to Know*, (2020).

community (the herd) became immune to the disease, the spread would stop.[55] Ferguson, like most experts, thought this strategy was too risky and recommended a suppression strategy. "In an unmitigated epidemic" the Imperial College team wrote, "we would predict approximately 510,000 deaths in Great Britain and 2.2 million in the US, not accounting for the potential negative effects on health systems being overwhelmed on mortality." They added that, "as early as the second week in April," bed capacity in critical-care wards would be exceeded. According to the *National Post* (April 11, 2020) "even under a best-case scenario, with strong public health measures in place, Canada may see 11,000 to 22,000 deaths before the pandemic is over." And in a worse-case scenario, the model used by Ottawa "showed deaths would easily top 300,000." A 75 percent reduction in personal contact rates would reduce deaths to under 46,000 in Canada. So far as Alberta was concerned, Premier Jason Kenney outlined for the *National Post* (April 8, 2020) a "probable scenario" that predicted 800,000 Albertans falling ill, and between 400 and 3,100 people dead. If the province did nothing, he went on, as many as 32,000 Albertans could die and 1.6 million could be infected. That same day, 1,373 cases had been diagnosed (not 1.6 million) and 26 Albertans had died (not 32,000).[56] World-wide, Ferguson and his team expected seven billion infections and 40 million deaths.[57]

The Imperial College team made some additional assumptions. First, there would be no COVID-19 vaccine available for 18 months (and they assumed that such a vaccine was needed). Second, anything other than suppression was equated with doing nothing so that special provisions to protect vulnerable members of the herd were ruled out. Third, they

---

[55] See Antonio Regalado, "What is Herd Immunity?" *MIT Technology Review*, (March 17, 2020); C. J. E. Metcalf et al., "Understanding Herd Immunity," *Trends in Immunology*, 36 (2015): 753–5; K.O. Kwok et al., "Herd Immunity," *Journal of Infection*, (March 18, 2020). We discuss the concept in more detail below.

[56] By mid-May, it was obvious that the Ferguson-Imperial College model was "consistently inaccurate and unreliable." Moreover, the model used to calculate Alberta deaths, its assumptions, method, and data, were still secret. Nor was it clear whether deaths *from* COVID-19 were distinguished from deaths *with* COVID-19, a problem that recurred in many jurisdictions. See Justice Centre for Constitutional Freedoms, "No Longer Demonstrably Justified: An Analysis of Alberta's COVID-19 Modelling," Justice Centre, Calgary, (May 13, 2020): 4, 20–21.

[57] Patrick G. T. Walker et al., "The Global Impact of COVID-19 and Strategies for Mitigation and Suppression," Imperial College, London, (March 26, 2020).

pointedly refused to consider "the ethical or economic implications" of either the suppression or the mitigation strategy. They added a few caveats regarding uncertainty and the need for extensive testing, but based on expected mortality alone, their model recommends that the only effective strategy to prevent large-scale deaths was suppression. Their conclusions sufficiently alarmed British Prime Minister Boris Johnson that he abandoned mitigation measures that were part of the herd-immunity strategy and imposed a national lockdown.

The first thing to recall about the Imperial College report is that it was based on a computer model. Models have long been used in social and natural science, and Ferguson was trained as a theoretical physicist, a discipline that is practically defined by models.[58] Moreover, models have been controversial for as long as they have been used. George Box, a well-known statistician, famously said "all models are wrong" for the simple reason that they are approximations, and they are based on assumptions whose validity is never self-evident. In economics, Paul Samuelson, whose economics textbook many of us studied as undergraduates and who was the first American to win a Nobel Prize in economics, once remarked that the most sophisticated market models correctly predicted nine of the past five recessions. His distinguished colleague on the left, J. K. Galbraith, agreed: economic modelling, Galbraith said, exists to make astrology look respectable. And biological models are far more complex than economic ones. From the outset, therefore, Canada and the rest of the world were "at the mercy of two data problems," one epidemiological, the other economic.[59]

In addition to the questionable reliability and validity of all models, one further attribute needs to be noted. Research physicians, immunologists, and virologists seek to resolve scientific puzzles, whereas epidemiologists pursue policy-related research. "Statistical modelling ... is pursued for the purpose of policy recommendation." The problem with such research is that in events involving an allegedly novel coronavirus, risks are incalculable in the literal sense that they cannot be calculated. The political purpose of such models is to create the perception "that either there was

---

[58] His thesis investigated "interpolations from crystalline to dynamically triangulated random surfaces," which seems rather removed from epidemiology save for the reliance of both discourses on modelling.
[59] Terence Corcoran, "At the Mercy of Two Data Problems," *Financial Post*, (April 6, 2020).

no uncertainty or the uncertainty was mitigated." In this respect, epidemiological models are akin to macroeconomic models or the models used by climatologists.[60] The fact is, there can be no scientific basis for making decisions when facing uncertainty. Dealing with risk depends on judgment, as Immanuel Kant explained in his third *Critique*, and there are no rules for the exercise of the power of judgment. There is only prudence.

On the surface, the model the Imperial College used looked adequate. It was a spatial model that divided the U.K. into small cells and then simulated various processes of transmission, incubation, and recovery for each cell. The model, called an assembly model, included a good deal of randomness and was run thousands of times to get a range of results that then were averaged. This is a common technique among modellers.

A closer look at the computer model by epidemiologists and computational biologists raised several troubling questions. First, Ferguson refused to publish the original source code and the ostensible owners of the code, namely Imperial College, refused a British *Freedom of Information Act* request on the grounds that there was no compelling public interest. Peter St. Onge remarked that Ferguson's code was unreliable and fragile, "giving different answers depending on the processing speed of the computer running the model."[61] Similarly, Chris von Csefalvay noted that the code was 13 years old, which is to say it was practically antique, and it was written to model an influenza pandemic. Moreover, thousands of lines of code were "undocumented," which meant it was impossible to take it apart and examine for errors — or to correct them. Accordingly, von Csefalvay wondered what the British government did to assess and validate the model, what safeguards they used to ensure it was correctly used, and so on. In his view, the code was "a tangled mess of undocumented steps." He concluded that only Ferguson's reputation, which he called "an incumbency effect," is what made the Imperial College model authoritative.[62] It would seem that the pandemic model effectively was as

---

[60] Reuven Brenner, "When Astrologers Rule," *Law and Liberty*, (June 9, 2020).

[61] Peter St. Onge, "The Worst-case Scenario that Closed Canada," *Financial Post*, (June 25, 2020). The processing speed depended on the complexity and size of the central processing units (CPUs) in the computers involved. That is, different computers would provide different results, rendering the results meaningless.

[62] Chris von Csefalvay, "The Unexamined Model is not Worth Trusting," *City Journal*, (May 15, 2020).

secret as the non-information coming from Wuhan and the WHO. Nevertheless, it served as the embodiment of power-knowledge.

Even the incumbency effect was built on questionable grounds. What Heather MacDonald called Ferguson's "apocalyptic" predictions had in the past proved to be gross exaggerations.[63] One earlier model predicted 150,000 deaths from mad-cow disease in 2002; the actual number of fatalities was 2,704. In 2005, Ferguson's model predicted 200 million deaths from avian flu; 455 persons actually died. Eventually, Ferguson was forced to resign from the British Scientific Advisory Group for Emergencies (SAGE), not because his COVID-19 model was so inaccurate as to be worthless but for a much more human failing: he was found to have violated the lockdown that he had so vocally supported for everyone else by entertaining a married woman, not his wife, in his London residence. After the fact, several commentators wondered why anyone listened to Ferguson in the first place. One can say the same of Tam and the WHO.

In all these instances, and in the examples of their provincial counterparts, the answer is the same: they were the experts. Who would not want to be governed by scientific expertise? For the experts and their supporters, that is a rhetorical question. As Donald G. McNeil Jr. wrote in the *New York Times*, experts "were united in the opinion that politicians must step aside and let scientists both lead the effort to contain the virus and explain to Americans what must be done." In fact, McNeil reported, the scientist he spoke with said "the microphone should not even be at the White House."[64] In reality, it is not at all obvious that experts should have the last word.

Granted, listening to experts is often advisable. On the other hand, "promising to heed their advice — in other words, to cede prudential judgment to technical experts — abrogates politics and evades responsibility."[65] The connection between apolitical expertise and

---

[63] Heather MacDonald, "A Short Guide to Justifying Re-Lockdown," *Spectator USA*, (May 25, 2020); see also Peter St. Onge, "The Flawed COVID-19 Model that Locked Down Canada," Montreal Economic Institute, Economic Notes: Health Policy Series, (June 2020).

[64] Donald McNeil, "The Virus Can be Stopped, but Only with Harsh Steps, Experts Say," *New York Times*, (March 22, 2020).

[65] Greg Weiner, "Expertise and Prudential Politics," *Law and Liberty*, (April 27, 2020).

progressive politics was present from the beginning of the progressive movement in the nineteenth century. It has the additional advantage for a progressive politician such as the current prime minister that he can claim, as he does, to be following the best available science. Foucault's power-knowledge, it seems to us, is clearly in play. For the experts, "having put so much effort into their work, it's also not unexpected and very human that most experts put a lot of weight on their conclusions and are convinced of their importance."[66] No one becomes an epidemiologist or a rocket scientist without years of focus on nothing else. But training and an ability to focus are not the sources of political prudence. That experts were the very antithesis of prudence is indicated in their eagerness not simply to give advice but to exercise their power-knowledge to make rules and ensure they were enforced — voluntarily if possible, but by compelling obedience if necessary.

One of the persistent curiosities regarding the success of moral entrepreneurs such as Ferguson in getting their interpretations into the public sphere and becoming authoritative is that other accounts were ignored. Statisticians and scientists at the University of Oxford, for example, developed a model with no apocalyptic implications, but the media have effectively ignored it. On March 17, 2020, John Ioannidis, whom the *Atlantic* identified a decade earlier as one of the most influential scientists alive, published a paper in *Statnews* saying that the data on COVID-19 were not sufficient or reliable enough to know the prevalence and fatality rate of the disease, nor which distancing and lockdown measures worked, and certainly provided no insight into what the downstream effects would be.[67] In late April, Scott Atlas, also at Stanford,

---

[66] John Lee, "Where is the Vigorous Debate about our Response to COVID?" *Spectator*, (April 12, 2020).

[67] John Ioannidis, "A Fiasco in the Making: As the Coronavirus Takes Hold, We are Making Decisions Without Reliable Data," *Statnews*, (March 17, 2020); see also Jeanne Lenzer and Shannon Brownlee, "Opinion: John Ioannidis and Medical Tribalism in the Era of COVID-19." Available at https://undark.org and Michael Schulson, "COVID-19 Prevalence: John Ioannidis Responds to his Critics," on *Undark*. Available at https://www.medscape.com/viewarticle/930646_print. The original preprint was published on May 5, 2020. John Ioannidis, Catherine Axfors, and Despina G. Contopoulos-Ioannidis, "Population-Level COVID-19 Morality Risk for Non-elderly Individuals Overall and for Non-elderly Individuals without Underlying Diseases in Pandemic Epicenters." Available at https://doi.org/10.1101/2020.0405.2254361.

told RealClear Politics that there was sufficient empirical data, along with knowledge of fundamental biology regarding viruses, to abandon the initial strategy of a lockdown for everyone, which by then was in full swing.[68] Early in June 2020, George Lundberg, M.D. raised the question: "Are patients dying 'From' COVID or 'With' COVID?"[69] A month later, Beda M. Stadler, a Swiss immunologist, made an even more fundamental argument, that "the coronavirus is slowly retreating" because "the immune response against the virus is much stronger than we thought."[70] There are, in other words, fundamental measurement problems that render the COVID-19 data highly questionable, not to say useless, even when the question of the deliberate exaggeration of the causes of death among patients is ignored.[71]

These papers — and there are numerous others available online — are all written by respected scientists, not internet trolls. Our point is not that they are correct and Ferguson and his allies and supporters are wrong. Rather, it is that, among qualified scientists, there is a debate, and that by and large, it has been unreported. Our question is: why?

One reason appears to be that grim prognostications always appear more prudent than optimistic ones. Apart from the frisson of horror at the contemplation of mega-deaths, if the grim prognosticator is wrong, he or she still looks prudent, whereas if one underestimates a threat, one looks irresponsible as well as wrong. The problem with grim prudence, however, is that an over-emphasis on nearly infinite vulnerabilities runs into the limit

---

[68] See Ian Schwartz, "Stanford University, Dr. Scott Atlas: Virus Panic Induced by Overestimation of Fatality Rate of Infected." (April 25, 2020). Available at https://realclearpolitics.com.

[69] http://www.medscape.com; see also Ross Clark, "Dying of COVID vs Dying with COVID," *Spectator USA*, (August 26, 2020).

[70] Beda Stadler, "Why Everyone was Wrong." Available at: www.worldhealth.net/news/why-everyone-was-wrong.

[71] For example, the federal Centers for Disease Control reported late in August that "for 6% of the deaths [reported], COVID-19 was the only cause mentioned."; Jack Davis, "CDC Now Says 94% of COVID Deaths had Underlying Condition, 6% were COVID Alone," *Western Journal*, (August 30, 2020); see also Joe Hoft," Shock Report: This Week CDC Quietly Updated COVID-19 Numbers: Only 9,210 American died from COVID-19 Alone, Rest had Different Other Serious Illnesses," *Gateway Pundit*, (August 29, 2020); Stephen Burgess, Mark J. Pensford, and Dipender Gill, "Are We Understanding Seroprevalence of SARS-CoV-2?" *BMJ*, (September 3, 2020), and references.

of finite resources. To put it another way, threats, like resources, are limited; vulnerabilities are not. When the media are filled with the ruminations of columnists masquerading as amateur epidemiologists, doomsday predictions and the demand for great sacrifices are as inevitable as the intended consequence: an enhanced moral panic.

One expression of this tendency is the cliché that over-reaction is better than under-reaction. How do the advocates of over-reaction know that? Well, they don't. What they claim is that "under-reaction," whatever that may be, will result in preventable deaths. But nobody knows that either. As a result, overreactors "find themselves in an enviable position. They're always right because they can never be proven wrong."[72] As we argue in section 5, the inevitable political consequence is that all political actors, along with the moral entrepreneurs, see the COVID-19 outbreak as a crisis and thus an opportunity to expand and consolidate their power-knowledge. And, as noted above, the emotion at the center of the message of the moral entrepreneurs is fear. Instead of promoting their ability to keep their citizens safe, governments (especially in Canada) tried to scare them and were successful, at least in the short term.

On sober reflection, it is obvious that government support of the prognostications and models of public health officials is not a testament to the validity of the models, opinions, or prognostications. That is, government support is hardly an endorsement of science. As we have argued, the models used to forecast the pandemic have nothing to do with science.[73] Even so, the certitude with which the public health establishment from WHO to health bureaucrats in Ottawa to the CDC in the U.S., have embraced a clearly flawed model is an index of how, in a panic, scientists and politicians and also the public are far more likely to accept certain untruth than uncertain truth.[74] That is the very definition of Foucault's regime of truth.

The result, as Andrew Potter noted in the *National Post* (May 30, 2020), is that Canadians "essentially turned the running of the country over to the public health experts, with political leaders at every level appearing more

---

[72] Jeffrey Polet, "Counting the Costs of Overreaction," *Law and Liberty*, (March 23, 2020).

[73] John Lee, "Where is the Vigorous Debate about the Response to COVID?"

[74] See the remarks of John Whyte, M.D., MPH, "Past Three Months of COVID Interviews: What We've Learned," (July 10, 2020). Available at: http://www.medscape.com.

than happy to let the country's various public-health officers take the lead."
As discussed below, there may have been intelligible reasons for this on
the part of the politicians, at least in the early stages of the pandemic when
no one (including the so-called experts) knew very much, but as noted
above, one would have expected these experts to have advanced more
modest and qualified recommendations had they been genuine scientists.
And there, precisely, is the problem with such experts; they are in fact
moral entrepreneurs: anyone who raises doubts, no matter how personally
and scientifically qualified the doubter may be, is accused of "arm-chair
quarter-backing, of impugning the integrity of public servants, or of
coming down from the hills to shoot the doctors while the battle is still
raging."[75]

For the so-called health experts themselves, their "newfound power
over almost the entirety of human life has been too exhilarating to give up
now." This is why any questioning of their power-knowledge has been
met by a new strategy to ensure the continuity of their future authority: the
"second wave" is bound to be worse (and it is coming!) if you, the people,
try to return to "normal." This is the new normal; get used to it. According
to WHO Chief Scientist Soumya Swaminathan, "so for a long time to
come, we have to maintain the same kind of measures that are currently
put in place." Perhaps indefinitely, because "we also don't know how long
these vaccines will protect for."[76] B.C. Provincial Health Officer Bonnie
Henry agreed (*Vancouver Sun*, September 11, 2020). No less an authority
than Tedros, the head of the WHO, said he could only "hope" the
pandemic would be over in two years (*National Post*, August 22, 2020). Or
as a *New York Times* headline (May 17, 2020) put it: "New Cases in US
Slow, Posing Risk of Complacency," which means: "do not stop being
fearful … while the virus risk may go down, complacency risk replaces it,
leaving us as threatened as before. The only proper posture is to shelter in
place permanently."[77] Tam echoed her American colleagues: Canada
cannot "relax too much too soon." The danger of complacency is at least
as large as the threat of COVID-19 (*National Post*, June 5, 2020). The only
exceptions to the advice to shelter in place on a permanent basis applied

---

[75] Andrew Potter, "Health Officials are Not Gods," *National Post*, (April 16, 2020).

[76] Carolyn Crist, "Pre-Covid Life May Not return Until 2022, WHO Scientist Says,"
Medscape, (September 16, 2020).

[77] Heather MacDonald, "A Short Guide to Justifying Re-lockdown," *Spectator USA*,
(May 25, 2020).

to individuals such as Ferguson, the prime minister, and MPs in Ottawa (*Globe and Mail*, September 11, 2020) and the mayor of Toronto. They knew and demonstrated that the danger of complacency did not apply to them. The prime minister justified taking a knee with thousands of others early in June with the following words: "To look out the window and see thousands upon thousands of young people, of Canadians of all ages stand in solidarity, wanting to see change happen, I felt it was important for me to be part of that. To be able to listen, to be able to hear people and to be able to understand and share with people how important it was to act" (*National Post*, June 9, 2020). Do as I say, not as I do, was their position.

To be specific, the three graces of public health officialdom in Canada, Tam, Deena Hinshaw, and Henry, respectively the chief public health officers of Canada, Alberta, and British Columbia, have become major celebrities. One can purchase T-shirts featuring images of the three of them. Hinshaw had a Facebook following of over 12,000 subscribers before its creator removed it because of an abundance of negative comments (CTV News, Edmonton, September 5, 2020). Many media pundits have called them heroines and they are trusted by many more of their fellow citizens than the political leaders they ostensibly advise. Thomas Baker, professor of communications at the University of Alberta, singled out Hinshaw for praise. She was "doing an excellent job of conveying the necessary expert opinion on the pandemic." He added: "In this pandemic, the experts are winning. The experts are maintaining their dominance as the place to go to get sound advice on which to base key decisions."[78] By the end of September, however, their images were sufficiently tarnished that they were targets of hostile and occasionally threatening messages (*National Post*, September 30, 2020). Something had changed, but what?

Consider: what, exactly, had they done? Historically, societies have quarantined infected individuals to protect the healthy general population from the spread of infectious diseases. These three, and their counterparts elsewhere in the world, have presided over "the first global quarantine of healthy populations in human history" and have done so by decree, by regulation, by ukase, and not by legislation or action that followed

---

[78] *National Post*, (April 3, 2020). Whether they are viewed as heroines or censorious scolds may be a matter of taste.

extensive political debate.[79] But from what has the general population been quarantined? From an otherwise faster spread of the virus, we are told. That was the point of instructions *urbi et orbi* to "flatten the curve" so that the health-care system would not be overwhelmed. There are two problems with this advice. First, the argument that COVID-19 would have caused millions of deaths absent the lockdown is a classic example of a *post hoc ergo propter hoc* fallacy. That is, it is impossible to tell if it worked.[80] Second, if the virus was present in the general population from late 2019, the rationale for the lockdown suddenly had the effect, among other things, of impeding the growth of herd immunity and eroding the robustness of individual immune systems.

As we argue in the next section, one of the consequences of deferring to public health officials has been, on their side, mission creep. No longer are such persons concerned with identifying, tracking, and investigating infectious or communicable diseases. Nowadays, their view of how much wine is OK to drink with dinner or what to do about income inequality can be justified as public health issues.[81] After downplaying the importance of wearing masks, Tam recently advised Canadians to wear masks while engaged in sexual intercourse (no kissing!) but added that "the lowest risk sexual activity during COVID-19 involves yourself alone." She did not say whether "involving yourself alone" involved any risk of going blind.[82] Perhaps next she will advocate "an eroticism of distance, a 'corona sutra,' with positions recommended by medical experts."[83] More seriously, the B.C. Centre for Disease Control issued a *COVID-19 Language Guide* that instructs the inhabitants of that province to avoid using the words infection, patient, risk, crisis, vulnerable, immigrant, drug abuse, detox,

---

[79] Peter Shawn Taylor, "Why We May Need to Lockdown Public Health Officials," *C2C*, (June 30, 2020).

[80] That does not mean that philosophically illiterate quants will not try to make a spurious case. They already have. See for instance, Ken Terry, "Shelter-in-Place Orders Averted Much Higher COVID-19 Death Toll," *Medscape*, (July 13, 2020).

[81] See Donald M. Berwick, M.D., "The Moral Determinants of Health," *Journal of the American Medical Association*, 324: 3 (July 12, 2020): 225–6. His conclusion, that "it is important and appropriate to expand the role of physicians and health care organizations into demanding and supporting societal reform," would be enthusiastically endorsed by many of his Canadian colleagues.

[82] *True North Wire*, (September 2, 2020).

[83] Pascal Bruckner, "Eros and Thanatos, Both Mashed," *City Journal*, (September 4, 2020).

born female, sex change, safe sex, penis, vagina, testicles, boyfriend, promiscuous, elderly, caregiver, handicapped, normal, prostitute, domestic violence, mental illness, convict, and obese, among others. Such words we are told are neither "culturally safe" nor respectful.[84] One must insist: the *COVID-19 Language Guide* was meant seriously.

---

[84] B.C. Centre for Disease Control, *BCCDC COVID-19 Language Guide: Guidelines for Inclusive Language for Inclusive Language for Written and Digital Content*, (Victoria: Provincial Health Services Authority, July 2020).

Pushback

One of the points John Ioannidis made in the paper discussed in the previous section contains some obvious common-sense observations. Because of limited testing capabilities in mid-March 2020, when his paper appeared, patients who tested positive for the virus were disproportionately those with severe symptoms leading to bad outcomes. At the time, there was only one example of a closed population that had been fully tested, the quarantined passengers of the cruise ship Diamond Princess. Aboard the vessel, the case fatality rate was one percent (at the time, the official projected WHO rate was 3.4 percent). The population tested was largely elderly and so susceptible to a higher death rate than the general population. When the Diamond Princess death rate was projected onto the age structure of the general population in the United States, it fell to 0.125 percent. Since the number of cases was small (seven deaths out of 700 passengers) the statistically adjusted death rate could have ranged, in the general population, from 0.025 percent to 0.625 percent. Since tourists may have different frequencies of chronic disease than the general population and since some of the (elderly) passengers may have died a short while later,[85] Ioannidis factored in those sources of uncertainty and concluded that "reasonable estimates for the case fatality ratio in the general U.S. population vary from 0.05% to 1%," with a "mid-range guess" of about 0.3 percent.[86]

This guess could be made more accurate if the prevalence of the infection by SARS-CoV-2 in a random sample of the general population were known and if the sampling were repeated at regular intervals in order to estimate more accurately the incidence of new infections. But those

---

[85] Even the apocalyptic Ferguson noted that as many as two-thirds of all those who died from COVID-19 during 2020 would likely have died by the end of the year anyway. This problem is another version of dying with, rather than from, COVID-19.

[86] John Ioannidis, "A Fiasco in the Making?" *Statnews,* (March 17, 2020).

data did not and do not exist. Worse, reliable data cannot exist because the number of infected persons "depends on the number of tests. The more tests you do, the more infected people you get."[87] The realities of fake data were ignored by the so-called experts in favour, as Ioannidis noted, for "prepare-for-the-worst" strategies that led "to extreme measures of social distancing and lockdowns. Unfortunately, we do not know if these measures work."[88] Moreover, we also cannot know if the strategy of "flattening the curve" worked because of collateral damage and other unanticipated consequences that are easily overlooked. These range from increased eating disorders, alcoholism, and mental health issues,[89] to increased and more intense crime patterns,[90] to greater opioid addiction and a greater number of fatal overdoses, which were exacerbated by the closed border with the U.S. because, evidently, less dangerous opioids came from American suppliers than Canadian ones.[91] Tam's response was to suggest the legalization of opioids and other hard drugs.[92] There is also

---

[87] Yoram Lass, "Nothing Can Justify this Destruction of People's Lives," *Spiked*, (May 22, 2020); see also Justin D. Silverman et al., "Using Influenza Surveillance Networks to Estimate State-specific Prevalence of SARS-CoV-2 in the United States," *Science Translational Medicine*, 12, (July 29, 2020).

[88] Ioannidis has long maintained that the effects of medical interventions are necessarily unknowable and that most research in support of such actions is (at best) highly questionable. See his "Why Most Published Research Findings are Fake," *PLOS Medicine*, 2:8. (2005); see also J. Bedford DeLong and Kevin Lang, "Are all Economic Hypotheses False?" *Journal of Political Economy*, 100:6 (1992): 1257–72. Ioannidis' paper is the most downloaded paper in the Public Library of Science, PLOS.

[89] Judi Kanne, "COVID Isolation, Anxiety 'Really Reinforce' Eating Disorders," *Medscape*, (August 13, 2020); Megan Brooks, "COVID-19 Shutdown Fuels Sharp Rise in Alcohol Abuse," *Medscape*, (September 29, 2020); Megan Brooks, "CDC Data Confirm Mental Health is Suffering During COVID-19," *Medscape*, (August 13, 2020).

[90] Marcus Felson et al., "Routine Activity Effects of the COVID-19 Pandemic on Burglary in Detroit, March 2020," *Crime Science*, 10 (June 23, 2020).

[91] Between January and June 2020, there were 261 deaths in Alberta from COVID-19 and 449 deaths from opioid overdoses. *National Post*, (September 26, 2020); see also Megan Brooks, "Surge in Opioid Overdoses Linked to COVID-19," *Medscape*, (September 21, 2020) for similar American data.

[92] *True North Wire*, (August 21, 2020); (August 26, 2020); *National Post*, (June 16, 2020); (August 24, 2020); Doyle Potenteau and Jon Azpiri, "Illicit Drug Deaths in BC Higher than Homicides, Car Crashes, Suicide, COVID-19 Combined: Report," *Global News*, (August 26, 2020).

evidence that heart attacks, strokes, illnesses leading to diabetic amputations, and other traumas have not been treated in an adequate or timely fashion.[93] Pets have also suffered: some gained weight from lack of exercise; others developed joint problems from too much exercise (*National Post*, September 10, 2020).

A second-order problem is the opportunity cost of devoting so much attention to COVID-19. Clinical trials for non-COVID-19-related medicines have just about ended.[94] In many hospitals, the anticipated surge in COVID-19 patients did not occur, but the hospitals still had to pay for excess and unused clinical capacity and patients suffered from the consequences of delay of diagnosis and treatment of their afflictions.[95] Anecdotal evidence from Canadian emergency departments suggests the same thing occurred here as in the U.S.[96] There are also anecdotal reports of unnecessary deaths from excessive wait-times *and* spontaneous recovery while on a wait-list.[97] The problem, as Zitner noted, is that "neither provincial health departments, nor the federal government are reporting this information." If data on who improved and who got worse while awaiting treatment were available, they would help avoid unnecessary and superfluous post-pandemic health-care delivery. Unfortunately for the experts, these data would also cast doubt on the wisdom of the lockdown and on the scientific expertise of those who advocated it.

There are other costs to be noted as well. Ioannidis observed, first of all: "We don't know how long social distancing measures and lockdowns can be maintained without major consequences to the economy, society, and mental health. Unpredictable evolutions may ensue, including financial

---

[93] See Debra Isaac and Paul W. M. Fedak, "Where Are All the Cardiac Patients?" *National Post,* (April 14, 2020); see also Randy Dotinga, "Diabetic Amputations Soared amid Italian Pandemic Lockdown," *Medscape*, (August 7, 2020).

[94] Debra L. Beck, "Non-COVID Clinical Trials Grind to a Halt During Pandemic," *Medscape,* (August 18, 2020).

[95] See Elizabeth Lawrence, "Nearly Half of Americans Delayed Medical Care due to Pandemic," *Kaiser Health News*, (May 22, 2020); David Zitner, "Assessing the 'Price of Caution' during the COVID-19 Pandemic," Commentary, Macdonald-Laurier Institute, (August 2020); Jody Zylke and Howard Buchner, "Mortality and Morbidity: The Measure of a Pandemic," *Journal of the American Medical Association*, (July 1, 2020).

[96] Debra Isaac and Paul W. M. Fedak, "Where are all the Cardiac Patients?"

[97] Sandeep Juhar, "People have Stopped Going to the Doctor: Most Seem Just Fine," *New York Times*, (June 22, 2020).

crisis, unrest, civil strife, war, and a meltdown of the social fabric." The most pessimistic scenario, which Ioannidis rejected, would see around 60 percent of the global population infected and one percent die, which matched the 1918 Spanish influenza pandemic.[98] The vast majority of deaths would come to persons with limited life expectancies, unlike the 1918 flu, which preferentially killed younger persons. His conclusion was also a common-sense one: "One can only hope that, much like 1918, life will continue. Conversely, with lockdowns of months, if not years, life largely stops, short-term and long-term consequences are entirely unknown and billions, not just millions, of lives may be eventually at stake."[99]

As noted above, Ioannidis is a professor of medicine, epidemiology, and population health at Stanford University's medical school. He drew out the social and political implications just discussed based on medical and epidemiological evidence. One of his most interesting views was: "I think that lockdowns and shutdowns have not really worked in the past. I do not think that the lockdown was what worked in China. I think that the lockdown happened after the epidemic wave had peaked."[100] To support his interpretation, he referred readers to the work of his Stanford colleague, Michael Levitt.

Levitt is a computational biologist — a numbers guy — who is also a Nobel Laureate in chemistry. In an early interview with the *Los Angeles Times* (March 23, 2020), he said that "what we need to control is the panic."[101] At the time, there was a lot of speculation about the possibility of an exponential growth of SARS-CoV-2 in the wake of Ferguson's report. Levitt pointed out that the virus can grow exponentially only when it is undetected and no one is trying to control it, neither of which conditions, he said, can ever obtain. A couple of days later, he addressed the Ferguson model directly. The number of deaths predicted for the outbreak on the Diamond Princess "is 59, more than eight times the actual

---

[98] Marcia Frellick, "COVID-19 and 1918 Flu Mortality 'In the Same Ballpark,'" *Medscape,* (August 13, 2020).
[99] See also Saurabh Jha, "John Ioannidis Explains his COVID Views," *Medscape,* (July 15, 2020).
[100] John Ioannidis, "Control Pandemic through Other Means," *National Post,* (August 14, 2020).
[101] Joe Mozingo, "Why this Nobel Laureate Predicts a Quicker Coronavirus Recovery," *Los Angeles Times,* (March 23, 2020).

number of seven ... The older passengers may die from old age: if we wait long enough, the Ferguson value will be accurate."[102]

In late June 2020, Levitt and his colleagues published a paper that generalized their findings from an analysis of the Chinese data.[103] They measured total numbers of deaths and total numbers of cases to get the death rate but also "the ratio of total cases (or deaths) ... for today divided by that of yesterday," which they called a "fractional change function" that measures the exponential growth of the death rate. Specifically, in Hubei on January 29 "the number of deaths today divided by that of yesterday was 1.3. Were such exponential growth of 30% a day to continue, everyone on earth would die within 90 days." So, obviously, exponential growth is not possible — and empirically, the fractional change declined to 18 percent by February 2. They found similar declines in all countries or regions, despite data inconsistencies regarding when a person was infected. That is, the ratios were consistent. As a result, a plateau date could be calculated, which would be followed by a decline.[104]

Among their conclusions: "It is evident from our data analysis that the growth of a COVID-19 epidemic does not follow an exponential growth law even in the very first days but instead its growth is slowing down exponentially through time." There are exceptions to this "simple law," particularly if many undetected infections are involved. To summarize the most startling conclusions of Levitt's argument: with outbreaks such as COVID-19, a similar mathematical pattern occurs whatever the interventions by governments. After about two weeks of exponential growth of cases and/or deaths, the growth becomes "sub-exponential." Levitt's discovery of this mathematical pattern matters because the Imperial College scenario assumed continued exponential growth without "mitigation." Levitt showed that such a scenario has not happened anywhere, including countries with minimal "mitigation" responses. Why

[102] Michael Levitt, "How Accurate are the Number of UK and US deaths Predicted by Ferguson et al.?" *Structural Biology*, Stanford School of Medicine, (March 25, 2020).

[103] Michael Levitt, Andrea Scaiewicz, and Francesco Zonta, "Predicting the Trajectory of any COVID-19 Epidemic from the Best Straight Line," *MedRXiv*, (June 30, 2020).

[104] For a confirmation of Levitt's general point that relied on economic arguments, see Andrew Atkeson, Karen Kopecky, and Tao Zha, "Four Stylized Facts about COVID-19," National Bureau of Economic Research, Working Paper 27719, (August 2020).

not? Levitt suggested that some degree of prior immunity and large numbers of asymptomatic cases were involved.[105] He has also suggested that "the virus seems to have this intrinsic property of not growing exponentially but actually growing slower and slower each day."[106]

There are social consequences to be reckoned with amid the collateral damage caused by the pandemic. The most obvious starts from the fact that the elderly and infirm are the most vulnerable to the virus and to the illness it brings with it; small businesses and wage labourers are the most economically exposed. The anticipated result is the consolidation and expansion not so much of political power aiming at tyranny but of economic and bureaucratic power-knowledge. The two orders of results are mutually reinforcing; with a compelling regime of truth, one size can be made to fit all. Just ask Procrustes. The consequences for age cohorts, however, are rather different. In reality, the age-specific effects of COVID-19 mean that public policies requiring all members of society to be treated in the same way invariably have a disproportionately malign effect on the young. Reducing risks to the relatively wealthy and powerful elderly members of society has been paid for by the younger members of society who are comparatively poor and powerless. As Craig Lerner observed, by imposing mandatory safety precautions on everybody, irrespective of age, we are being "geriatric and cowardly."[107] The possible consequences of this form of intergenerational injustice have seldom ever been noted.[108] Let's make an attempt.

The context may be outlined by the question of over-reaction. A sensible reaction, as Aristotle observed (EN, VI:2), requires proper

---

[105] See his interview in the *Stanford Daily*, (August 2, 2020), and Donna Rachel Edmonds, "Nobel Laureate: Surprised if Israel Has More than 10 Coronavirus Deaths," *Jerusalem Post*, (March 20, 2020). With close to 900 deaths by late August, this estimate was wrong. So far as we can tell, he has not addressed the matter. By mid-September, the Israeli government ordered a three-week lockdown. See *Stratfor*, (September 18, 2020).

[106] Interview, *Stanford Daily*, (May 4, 2020); Sharon Kirkey, "Give Me Liberty or Give Me COVID-19," *National Post*, (May 23, 2020); see also Therese Borden, "Sleepless in the Pandemic," *Medscape*, (July 30, 2020).

[107] Craig S. Lerner, "Who's Being Mature about COVID-19 Risks?" *Law and Liberty*, (July 22, 2020).

[108] See Patrick Lynch, "COVID's Age Discrimination," *Law and Liberty*, (September 17, 2020). According to Lynch, the median net worth of Americans over 65 is $250,000; for those under 35, it is $25,000.

reasoning, which in turn requires sufficient information and experience — and the absence of fear. "The combination of fear and ignorance typically leads to panic and hysteria, both extreme manifestations of over-reaction."[109] It also helps in insuring that over-reaction, however it is measured, is acceptable because one doesn't have much at stake: if one can work at home and order take-out, one can afford to overreact. People who otherwise would serve you in a restaurant have other things to be concerned about, such as paying rent. That is, for many Canadians, losing their job or their business is far more frightening than contracting the virus. But not for those in the knowledge class — the "experts," the journalists, and the politicians. They are precisely the advocates of over-reaction and the most resistant to cost-benefit analysis. No one wants Granny to die, but we still need to compare mortality rates with unemployment rates. That is, whether we like it or not, we are bound to balance the health risk of persons with attenuated lifespans — Granny — with economic well-being for younger members of society. The notion that "one life might be saved" by locking down the economy is ridiculous. People die. Old people die more often than young ones. The demands of one generation upon another cannot be avoided and consequences with respect to justice, however they are worked out, are never equally distributed. As Gwyn Morgan observed: "In hindsight, keeping healthy workers away from their jobs — the first such quarantine ever undertaken — may be the most damaging decision in Canadian history."[110] So much seems self-evident to us.

As we discuss in detail in section six, the Canadian government's response and, presumably, the opinion of the alleged experts upon whom it relied was, in Trudeau's words, to do "whatever it takes" to ward off the pandemic. Such a policy was the inevitable consequence of the belief that saving lives, whether that of Granny in an assisted-living home in High River or her grandson, an unemployed welder in Fort McMurray, was priceless in the literal sense of being beyond price. Unfortunately, such

---

[109] Jeffrey Polet, "Counting the Costs of Overreaction."

[110] Gwyn Morgan, "The Lockdown Contrarians were Right," *C2C*, (June 10, 2020). The obvious and differential impact of the lockdown on younger and older Canadians may explain why a Leger poll for the Association of Canadian Studies (*National Post*, September 16, 2020) showed that Albertans, with a younger demographic, were more likely to believe that health officials exaggerated the threat of COVID-19, especially to younger people.

statements and others with similar meaning are untrue. Economists, including those in the government of Canada, have long put dollar values on an individual life.[111] But as Terence Corcoran said in mid-May, he was unaware of any work that made a cost-benefit analysis of the country's anti-COVID-19 operation, so he gave it a shot using a well-known (at least to economists) "value of a statistical life" or VSL.[112] The result, Corcoran said, could only be a general estimate because the data were supplied by the same two highly unreliable and widely debated disciplines, one economic, the other epidemiological. One obvious implication is that if the government attempted to argue that their massive intervention with the lockdown was worthwhile because the cost to the economy was less than the value of life saved, they didn't know what they were talking about. Why? Because "all such benefit claims remain doubtfully based on an equation linking two artificial constructs: Total benefit = number of lives saved x value of a life."[113] Even if the value of a statistical life is accepted, the infection/fatality rate remains completely unknown, partly because there have been insufficient tests done, but more importantly because in a dynamic situation today's test result might be different tomorrow. As a consequence, the costs of the lockdown will be real and high, but the benefits will be mostly statistical and abstract.

A few weeks after Corcoran's effort, Herbert Grubel, an economist at Simon Fraser University, made a more ambitious cost-benefit analysis of Canada's response to the pandemic.[114] According to the International Monetary Fund (IMF), Grubel said, by June government lockdown policies had cost the national GDP about $113 billion. This figure did not include extra public expenditures — CERB, corporate and wage subsidies, etc. — which may not lead to lower short-term output but do add to the

---

[111] Treasury Board Secretariat. *Canadian Cost-Benefit Analysis Guide: Regulatory Proposals*, (Ottawa: Treasury Board Secretariat, 2007).

[112] For details, see the early and classic work of Kip Viscusi, "The Value of Risks to Life and Health," *Journal of Economic Literature*, 31 (1993): 1912–46; or Thomas Kniesner and Viscusi, "The Value of a Statistical Life," *Oxford Research Encyclopedia of Economics and Finance*, Preprint, (May 16, 2019).

[113] Terence Corcoran, "The Price of Life," *Financial Post*, (May 15, 2020); see also Terence Corcoran, "The Precautionary Disaster," *Financial Post*, (June 25, 2020); and Terence Corcoran, "Time to take Banal Clichés off the Table," *Financial Post*, (March 25, 2020).

[114] Herbert Grubel, "The Costs and Benefits of Canada's Pandemic Response," *C2C*, (June 21, 2020).

public debt, making the total cost around $226 billion. Despite its many flaws, of which Grubel was aware, he used the high estimates of the Ferguson-Imperial College model as the basis of calculating deaths avoided, which was conceptualized as the chief benefit of government policy. Given the model's overestimation of deaths, it would also overestimate benefits. As noted above, the model predicted four deaths per 1,000 population absent "non-pharmaceutical interventions" (i.e., physical distancing, quarantining, etc.). By taking such precautions, the death rate would be halved. By mid-June 2020, when Grubel's analysis appeared, the number of deaths in Canada was about 8,300. According to the Ferguson model, the same number of deaths would have been prevented. On the other hand, Grubel calculated that about 2,100 suicides could be directly attributed to the COVID-19 pandemic.[115] That works out to around 6,200 as a net estimate of deaths prevented. If the $226 billion figure is accepted, the cost of saving each life is $36 million or so. Grubel then raised the obvious question: Is this a good deal?

To answer it, he used the federal government's VSL figure developed in 2004, and thus prior to the COVID-19 outbreak, of $6.1 million, which works out to about $8 million today. (To simplify, Grubel ignored the question of age; the actual cost of GDP contraction is higher for younger Canadians but more deaths per capita have come to older ones). The question the model raises, however valid or questionable the assumptions that sustain it, is simple. Is what Canada has done a good way of saving lives or could more lives have been saved by doing things differently? One thing is obvious: expenditures upward of $36 million a life greatly exceeds the federally accepted VSL of $8 million. Grubel's conclusion seems reasonable enough: "Canada's experience explicitly fails the requirement of sound, cost-effective public policy as demonstrated by our simple cost/benefit analysis." This is the financial context within which the Swedish alternative, discussed in section 5, is considered.

The views of public health officials, who cannot be expected to know anything about economics (and who, time and again, have shown themselves to be economic ignoramuses), nevertheless have social, economic, and political consequences. Interestingly enough, these medical experts seem oblivious to the problem of mission creep. For example, the initial exhortation of "flatten the curve," was intended to ensure that the

---

[115] *National Post*, (June 4, 2020).

health-care system did not collapse under the pressure created by massive numbers of COVID-19 patients in the emergency rooms of hospitals across the country. This threat never materialized, a point made both in the mainstream and independent media.[116] Alberta, for example, reserved over 2,000 beds for COVID-19 patients. By April 30, 2020, 90 were filled. British Columbia did better (or worse), reserving 2,400 beds and filling 79. Only Quebec has had a problem. No one knows why — or if they do, no one says why, though iatrogenic or nosocomial infection seems an obvious explanation.

In response to the success achieved in flattening the curve, politicians and health-care officials have moved on to more ambitious objectives. As Kevin Libin observed, they now seek to stop persons from contracting COVID-19 altogether.[117] Mission creep is the vocational temptation of all bureaucratic experts, but in the context of the pandemic it is symbiotically linked to what Matthew Crawford has called "safetyism," a sentiment wherein "the safer we become, the more intolerable any remaining risk appears."[118] Because no one can ever be completely safe, there is no limit to the expanding imperium of bureaucrats inspired or armed with this perniciously benevolent ideology. The result, as we have already seen, has been to reinforce "a moral-epistemic apparatus in which the experts are to rule over citizens conceived as fragile incompetents," which, to reiterate what is by now obvious, is the whole point of power-knowledge. Nowhere is this more obvious than in the shifting counsels of experts regarding the wearing of masks.

On June 1, 2020, the Association of American Physicians and Surgeons (AAPS) published a five-page document, "Mask Facts," that summarized the transmission vectors of the SARS-CoV-2 virus and the utility of several kinds of masks in intercepting respiratory droplets. A properly fitted N95 respirator effectively blocks 95 percent of tiny (down to 0.3 microns or micrometres) particles; hence the name. Unfortunately, it also impairs breathing, reduces blood oxygenation (hypoxia), and increases blood CO_2 (hypercapnia), which means it can cause the wearer to pass out. Surgical

---

[116] See Raymond de Souza, *National Post*, (May 23, 2020); Alberta Institute, (April 29, 2020).

[117] Kevin Libin, "Politicians Paralyzed with Fear," *National Post*, (May 5, 2020).

[118] Matthew Crawford, "The Danger of Safetyism" *Unherd*, (May 15, 2020); see also Heather MacDonald, "The Paranoid Style in COVID-19 America," *Spectator USA*, (April 27, 2020).

masks, designed to protect patients during surgery from respiratory droplets from a surgeon, also reduce blood-oxygen levels, the longer such a mask is worn, the greater the reduction in blood oxygen. Hypoxia is also associated with increased risks from cancer, inflammation, heart attack, and stroke, as well as such minor complaints as "dry-eye syndrome" (*National Post*, September 10, 2020). Moreover, if you are infected with COVID-19 — wearing a mask, particularly if it fits tightly on the face the way an N95 is supposed to do — you will be constantly rebreathing the virus and thus concentrating it in your nose.

The conclusion, "wearing masks will not reduce SARS-CoV-2" reiterated the conclusion of a 2012 study of the effectiveness of masks in preventing flu transmission.[119] The use of T-shirts, scarves, cloth masks, towels and so on are even less effective than masks. They are little more than the expression of a fashion statement but carry the additional risk that reuse and poor filtration may increase the chances of infection. The 2020 AAPS study suggested by way of conclusion that "in many cases, the desire for widespread masking is a reflexive reaction to anxiety over the pandemic." This summary interpretation echoed a study published in the authoritative *New England Journal of Medicine* a week or so earlier.[120] That study began by noting that "wearing a mask outside health care facilities

---

[119] Faisal bin-Reza et al., "The Use of Masks and Respirators to Prevent Transmission of Influenza: A Systematic Review of the Scientific Evidence," *Influenza and other Respiratory Viruses*, 6 (2012): 257–67; in October, 2019 the WHO reported that the wearing of facemasks has "limited" effectiveness ("Non-Pharmaceutical Public Health Measures for Mitigating Risk and Impact of Epidemic and Pandemic Influenza); see also John Miltmore, "Europe's Top Health Officials Say Masks Aren't Helpful in Beating COVID-19," Foundation for Economic Education, (August 6, 2020). A subsequent study noted that masking is associated with lower transmission between infected patients and front-line healthcare workers, but said nothing about masking the general population. See S. Schaeffer Spires and Valeria Fabre, "Studies Track Infections to Measure Mask Effectiveness," *Medscape*, (August 14, 2020). Even Bonnie Henry, B.C.'s provincial health officer, allowed that masks were "the end of our hierarchy of controls. The least effective of the layers we need," Lindsay Shepherd, interview, *True North*, (August 11, 2020). A highly qualified and tentative endorsement of masking is made by Monica Gandhi and George W. Rutherford, "Facial Masking for COVID-19: Potential for 'Variolation' and We Await a Vaccine," *New England Journal of Medicine*, (September 8, 2020).

[120] Michael Klompas et al., "Universal Masking in Hospitals in the Covid-19 Era," *New England Journal of Medicine*, 382:21 (May 21, 2020).

offers little, if any, protection from infection" and that in many cases, wearing a mask is just an expression of anxiety.[121] The authors also noted that there may be "additional benefits" that have nothing to do with reducing pathogen spread. Mask-wearing, for instance, "may remind people" of the importance of physical distancing and other measures, which is a polite way of saying that mask-wearing is virtue-signaling.[122] Or as Tedros, the WHO boss said: "By wearing a mask, you're sending a powerful message to those around you that we're all in this together."[123]

The authors of the *New England Journal of Medicine* study added that "it is also clear that masks serve symbolic roles." Specifically, these talismans may increase the perception of safety among health-care workers who wear masks and increase trust in the hospital administrators that they are taking care of their employees. "Although such reactions may not be strictly logical," the authors conclude, "we are all subject to fear and anxiety, especially during times of crisis" so that what may be from a medical perspective a "marginally beneficial" mask may make a much greater contribution in reducing "the transmission of anxiety." Since none of the authors of this paper is a specialist in fear, anxiety, or other psychological disorders, it is fair to say that, in addition, masks may also serve other "symbolic roles."

Before considering what they may be, let us note that there is one obvious way to determine if masks have any effect outside the hospital context — in hairdressing salons, grocery stores, or bars, for example. This would be to conduct what is called a "human challenge study" and compare the effectiveness of masks in reducing the transmission of the virus to healthy persons. Such an experiment would entail having infected individuals transmit SARS-CoV-2 by coughing on uninfected ones. Some of the infected subjects would be wearing masks, some not, and likewise with the recipients. If the uninfected recipients were young and healthy

---

[121] Bridget Balch, "The Science and Psychology behind Masking to Prevent the Spread of COVID-19," *Association of American Medical Colleges News*, (July 30, 2020). Yet another study showed that surgical procedure masks with ear loops were about 38 percent effective as long as the wearer didn't move her head — then effectiveness dropped to 21 percent for three-micron particles. Megan Brooks, "Surgical, Procedure Masks Likely Okay in Routine Care," *Medscape*, (August 11, 2020).

[122] See the unintentionally comic discussion of mask-wearing etiquette in the *National Post*, (July 25, 2020).

[123] *National Post*, (August 22, 2020).

volunteers, the medical risk would be minimal. When Matthew Parris proposed such an experiment to British medical practitioners, he was told that such a common-sense experiment would be prohibited on ethical grounds.[124] That is, human challenge trials were opposed by the experts, not the potential volunteers because, the experts said, there were too many unknowns with the SARS-CoV-2 virus for volunteers to give informed consent. In other words, the bureaucrats in the WHO and national governments would decide such matters, not individuals who were willing to take responsibility for risk.[125] These ethically sensitive medical persons did not seem to understand that by not conducting a human challenge study on a population of healthy volunteers, they were in fact conducting a human challenge study on the general population who did not volunteer. By late October, the experts have changed their minds and, despite their misgivings, allowed challenge trials to proceed in the U.K. (*National Post*, October 21, 2020).

The discussion regarding masks might also have been more rational and conducted at a lower decibel level if the so-called experts had not changed their minds on the alleged benefits. Up to May 20, 2020, for example, Tam argued that the incorrect use of masks could increase the spread of the virus, which is also what her scientific colleagues argued; after May 20, she advocated universal mask-wearing whether the wearer was competent or not.[126] Whatever the argument for the use of masks in hospitals, the advocacy of the universal use of masks necessarily increased the power-knowledge of the advocates. Thus, for example, the *Calgary Herald* (June 20, 2020) carried a story that some physicians in the city favoured compulsory use of masks. One of them, Joe Vipond, was named as an "organizer with the Alberta chapter of the Masks4Canada advocacy group." In the same story, Fuyo Watanabe, who co-founded the "Mask Makers YYC" group in March, complained that "demand is slowing down for the acceptance of masks in public; people just aren't wearing masks as

---

[124] Matthew Parris, "In an Age of Science, Why are Face Masks a Matter of Opinion?" *Spectator USA*, (July 23, 2020).

[125] Kathleen Doheny, "Are Human Challenge Trials for COVID-19 Vaccine Worth the Risk?" *Medscape*, (August 7, 2020).

[126] In the U.S., the incumbent of the equivalent position to Tam, Anthony Fauci, likewise changed his mind on the efficacy of hydroxychloroquine in treating coronaviruses both therapeutically and prophylactically. See *True Pundit*, (July 12, 2020).

frequently." Hence the need to make mask-wearing mandatory. Late in July 2020, Calgary city council joined a couple of cities in Laurentian Canada and passed a bylaw making mask-wearing compulsory in public buildings. Edmonton followed on August 1, but, as in Calgary, exemption cards were made easily available, mainly because compulsory masking was likely to violate Canadians' *Charter* rights.[127] But then, when too many Edmontonians obtained exemption cards, the program was "paused" a couple of weeks after it began owing to "abuse of the program from residents who don't have a legitimate exemption." There was an inconclusive discussion of what constituted a "legitimate exemption." Then, on August 24, Glenn Millar filed a statement of claim in the Alberta Court of Queen's Bench suing the City of Edmonton for $565 million because of the public health danger posed by discarded used masks.[128] Neither politicians nor journalists seem to think these events odd.

Given the medical evidence that the benefit of mask-wearing is chiefly symbolic and the supporting arguments entirely anecdotal,[129] one might ask: What is the symbolism associated with the imposition of the opinions of the alleged experts, including Tam, Hinshaw, Henry, and now Vipond

---

[127] See "Mask Exemptions Being Issued for Edmonton Residents," CTV News, (August 9, 2020); the Justice Centre, "Mandatory Masking Requirements Represent an Interference with Personal Autonomy," press release, (July 2, 2020). A family of four was removed by the Calgary Police Service from WestJet Flight 652, the red-eye bound for Toronto, on September 9, 2020 because the 19-month-old family member became hysterical and threw up when she was forced to wear a mask. Transport Canada regulations exempt children under age two. WestJet was sufficiently rattled by the incident that they cancelled the flight and no one got to fly. *National Post*, (September 10, 2020).

[128] Dustin Cook, "City of Edmonton Facing $565-Million Lawsuit over COVID-19 Mandatory Mask Law," *Edmonton Journal,* (August 26, 2020).

[129] See, for example, Nina Bai, "Still Confused about Masks? Here's the Science behind How Face Masks Prevent Coronavirus," *University of California, San Francisco, News,* (June 26, 2020). UCSF is the chief medical school in the California system. Among other things recommended to "prevent" coronavirus, the author mentions using "a damp washcloth." Mayo Clinic Staff, "COVID-19: How Much Protection do Face Masks Offer?" *MFER,* (July 17, 2020), noted that masks "help slow the spread of the virus" when "combined with other preventive measures such as frequent hand-washing and social distancing." If true, that says nothing about the effectiveness of mask-wearing on its own. Caitlin McCabe, "Face Masks Really Do Matter: The Scientific Evidence is Growing," *Wall Street Journal,* (July 27, 2020). In short, such evidence is entirely anecdotal.

and Watanabe? It seems to us that anxiety and fear are the experiences that mask-wearing is intended to evoke. Masks also confer a degree of anonymity compared to a mask-free face, suggesting that, as the experts and the politicians say, "we're all in this together." There is another aspect of masking that seldom is noted and never emphasized. In *Lord of the Flies*, one group of boys turns themselves into fanatics who are terrified of the invisible enemy and hide their own identities with masks. "The mask was a thing of its own," William Golding wrote, "behind which Jack hid, liberated from shame and self-consciousness." So adorned, they developed rituals that will keep "the Beast" away. As Patrick Fagan observed, in the present context with the current "invisible enemy,"[130] face masks are simply "an extension of lockdown to the outside world — they serve to keep us socially and psychologically distanced from our fellow man." He raised the question: What do you think the psychological consequences of wearing a face mask will be? Hint: "There is a reason masks are worn chiefly by anarchists, criminals and perverts." When the emphasis for mask-wearing is on virtue-signaling that indicates the wearer's enthusiasm to defeat the "invisible enemy" by indicating one's own purity, it should be no surprise that maskers become sadistic puritans, ready to censure their fellow citizens.[131]

Finally, one must note that this bureaucratic preference for collectivism, with experts commanding collective behaviour by making masking compulsory, turns the mask into a "symbol of subjugation."[132] Notice as well that because the mask covers the mouth it constitutes, again symbolically, the silencing of the wearer. Moreover, in fact it is often difficult to understand the speech of a masked man or woman. Mask wearing, in short, is the behavioural expression of just what the experts always seek: a fearful and docile population that does what it is told by its betters.

---

[130] See also Tino Delamerced, "COVID's War Rhetoric is Harmful to Med Students," *Medscape*, (September 1, 2020).

[131] Patrick Fagan, "The Lockdown Lobotomy," *The Critic*, (August 11, 2020). On the other hand, in Japanese culture there is a flirtatious notion called chirarism, from the word chirari, meaning a "glimpse." As Gary Dexter explained, "it means covering in order to suggest uncovering. Hiding the face stimulates the erotic imagination in Japan." Perhaps something similar is taking place in grocery stores in Canada? See Dexter, "Why the Japanese Love Wearing Facemasks," *Spectator USA*, (September 18, 2020).

[132] Heather MacDonald, "A Short Guide to Justifying Re-Lockdown."

Let us consider one additional controversy or dispute among experts: the efficacy of hydroxychloroquine, HCQ, as a treatment for SARS-CoV-2 infection. The initial controversy centered on Didier Raoult, a French clinical physician who was also a medical scientist. He had successfully treated patients using HCQ, an off-patent drug that was conventionally used to treat lupus, arthritis, and malaria, among other afflictions. He treated his patients with HCQ in conjunction with zinc and a bacterial antibiotic, azithromycin. These drugs could be administered at exceptionally low cost, having been in use for decades. On May 12, 2020, a very unflattering piece on Raoult appeared in the *New York Times*. The author called him an oracle, a Napoleonic personality, a narcissist with a "marble statue of himself," a contrarian with a "tight contemptuous mouth" and "funny hair." He believed "that science, and life, ought to be a fight," and he published too much. In addition, he was skeptical of the utility of mathematical models in epidemiology and was dismissive of the alarmism that constituted the default response of infectious-disease experts. "This anguish over epidemics," Raoult wrote, "is completely untethered from the reality of deaths from infectious diseases." His real sin for the *Times*, however, was that President Donald Trump liked his use of HCQ as a treatment for COVID-19.[133]

On May 5, 2020, Raoult and his team published in *Travel Medicine and Infectious Diseases* their study of the "Early Treatment of COVID-19 Patients with Hydroxychloroquine and Azithromycin: A Retrospective Analysis of 1061 Cases in Marseille, France."[134] The day before it appeared, Raoult testified before the French National Assembly that the article had been refused by the *Lancet* the same week the British publication accepted a study highly critical of HCQ.[135] In the June 5 edition of the *Lancet*, the authors of this piece said they were unable to provide the data on which the negative conclusions regarding HCQ were based and the journal issued a retraction.

One of the criticisms made in the *New York Times* article that was repeated by critics such as Anthony Fauci was that Raoult's results were

---

[133] Scott Sayare, "He was a Science Star: Then He Promoted a Questionable Cure for COVID-19," *New York Times*, (May 12, 2020).

[134] The paper was submitted on May 1, 2020.

[135] Mandeep Mehra et al., "Hydroxychloroquine or Chloroquine with or without a Macrolide for Treatment of COVID-19: A Multinational Registry Analysis," *Lancet*, (May 22, 2020) (this was the date of the print edition).

"anecdotal." This description was based on the fact that HCQ had not undergone random control tests or random control trials (RCTs). As Raoult explained to the *Times*: "We're not going to tell someone, 'Listen, today's not your lucky day; you're getting the placebo; you're going to be dying.'" Such trials, Raoult told the *Times*, appeal to statisticians, whom he dismissed as "methodologists who have never seen a patient."[136] Or, as he said more politely in the *Travel Medicine* paper, "in our analysis, which is not an RTC but which related the real-life experience of physicians testing patients in the context of an emerging pandemic," they reported the outcomes of treating COVID-19 patients with "an HCQ+AZ (Azithromycin and Zinc) combination from the time of diagnosis."

A couple of comments are in order. First, it is simply a fact that many useful developments in public health have never been validated by RCTs. This alternative is often referred to as the parachute paradigm: we accept that parachutes reduce injury to people who jump from airplanes even though the effect has never been proven in a randomized control trial comparing survival rates of jumpers with parachutes to those without. Second, RCTs usually take years to complete, and under the emergency conditions of an emerging pandemic, following the standard protocol for drug development would simply increase the number of infections and deaths: "Today's not your lucky day." Third, neither Raoult nor anyone else ever claimed that using HCQ by itself and not in conjunction with azithromycin and zinc was effective. Thus using it alone in randomized controlled trials was guaranteed to end in failure. And fourth, members of Raoult's team were explicit about the limited usefulness of his HCQ treatment: "We know that in acute viral diseases, the earlier you treat, the better your chances of success. It makes no sense to include people who are at the edge of death in the study. We're not claiming to be able to treat people who are nearly dead."[137]

---

[136] Interestingly enough, while hydroxychloroquine may have been discounted by the public health experts, that did not prevent other health-care professionals, such as front-line physicians, from offering large amounts of the drug for "office use," which included use by the physicians for personal and family members. One of the effects was to create shortages for those patients who used it for approved treatments of malaria, lupus, and rheumatoid arthritis. *National Post*, (April 7, 2020).

[137] Quoted in Elizabeth Woodworth, "The Media Sabotage of Hydroxychloroquine Use for COVID-19: Doctors Worldwide Protest the Disaster," *Global Research*,

Raoult also accused his critics of being apologists for "big pharma." The argument was, obviously, circumstantial. Clinical trials are normally financed and undertaken by large drug companies, often at the request of national health agencies. "It is in this political-industrial movement that evidence-based medicine and its statistical methods of randomization have been established, giving the illusion of a mathematical demonstration that cannot be falsified."[138] In the context of the current pandemic, it is obviously in the interests of large drug companies to convince governments, health-care officials, and the general population that it is better to wait for suitably randomized, control-tested vaccines, however long that takes. Raoult, a clinical practitioner, thought that such delay violated his Hippocratic oath.

Around the same time, a Yale professor of epidemiology, Harvey Risch, made essentially the same argument as his French colleague. HCQ and AZ, as well as HCQ and doxycycline (an antibiotic), "are generally safe for short-term use in the early treatment of most symptomatic high-risk outpatients, where not contraindicated, and that they are effective in preventing hospitalization for the overwhelming majority of such patients." Moreover, if these combined medications were regularly used with such patients; that is, symptomatic, high-risk outpatients whose infection had been discovered early in the progress of the disease, it was "likely" that "an enormous number of lives" would be saved. "It is our obligation," he said, "not to stand by, just 'carefully watching' as the old and infirm and inner-city of us are killed by this disease and our economy is destroyed by it and we have nothing to offer except high-mortality hospital treatment." HCQ + AZ and HCQ-doxycycline (preferably with zinc) may not work, "but urgency demands that we at least start to take that risk and evaluate what happens, and if our situation does not improve we can stop it, but we shall know that we did everything that we could

---

(June 30, 2020). Raoult would not have been surprised when, in an effort to discredit HCQ, several pharma-connected individuals discovered, using an RCT, that HCQ by itself was ineffective. See B. S. Abella et al., "Efficacy and Safety of Hydroxychloroquine vs Placebo for Pre-exposure SARS-CoV-2 Prophylaxis among Health Care Workers," *JAMA Internal Medicine*, (September 30, 2020).
[138] Laurent Mucchielli, "Behind the French Controversy over the Medical Treatment of COVID-19: The Role of the Drug Industry," *Journal of Sociology*, (June 17, 2020).

instead of sitting by and letting hundreds of thousands die because we did not have the courage to act according to our rational calculation."[139]

Risch's article drew a critical comment and a subsequent response by him.[140] On August 12, he published an op-ed in the *Washington Examiner* that introduced some additional political issues. "To date," he reiterated, "there are no studies whatsoever, published or in pre-print, that provide scientific evidence against the treatment approach for high-risk outpatients that I have described." The consequence of using outpatient data from patients already hospitalized and for the most part already very sick "to block emergency use of petitions for outpatient use" of HCQ and additional medicines, was "a serious and unconscionable mistake." Worse, so far as Risch was concerned, was the politicization of HCQ, much as the *New York Times* did with Raoult. Fauci, he said, "has implied that I am incompetent … A group of my Yale colleagues has publicly intimated that I am a zealot who is perpetuating a dangerous hoax and conspiracy theory."[141]

That a dissenting view, backed by evidence and argument, on the question of HCQ's efficacy should be understood by Risch's colleagues at the Yale Medical School as evidence that he had embraced a conspiracy theory and a hoax is pretty clear evidence of the presence and persuasiveness of a moral panic. The same thing happened late in July when a group of doctors held a "white-coat summit" on the steps of the U.S. Supreme Court.[142] Alison Meek, a history professor at Western

---

[139] Harvey A. Risch, "Opinion: Early Outpatient Treatment of Symptomatic, High-Risk COVID-19 Patients that should be Ramped-Up Immediately as Key to the Pandemic Crisis," *American Journal of Epidemiology*, (May 27, 2020).

[140] Vincent Fleury, "Comment on 'Early Outpatient Treatment,'" *American Journal of Epidemiology*, (July 20, 2020); Harvey Risch, "Response to Critics," *American Journal of Epidemiology*, (July 20, 2020).

[141] Harvey Risch, "Hydroxychloroquine Works in High-Risk Patients and Saying Otherwise is Dangerous," *Washington Examiner*, (August 12, 2020). In Canada, Paul Alexander was pilloried by his orthodox medical colleagues for questioning whether RTCs are always the "gold standard." *National Post*, (September 16, 2020). He didn't mention parachutes.

[142] "Docs Fight Back against Conspiracy Theories," *Medscape*, (August 5, 2020). Consider also an early and relatively moderate attempt to think clearly about the question: Paraminder Dhillon et al., "COVID-19 Breakthroughs: Separating Fact from Fiction," *Federation of European Biochemical Societies Journal*, 287 (2020): 3612–32.

explained that questioning the experts seemed to her to be prima facie evidence of believing in conspiracies, which she explained by the observation that conspiracies provide such questioners with a sense of "community."[143] In a similar explanatory vein, Aengus Bridgman and his political science colleagues at McGill argued that "exposure to social media is associated with misperceptions regarding basic facts about COVID-19 while the inverse is true for news media," which is to say orthodox mainstream media. Of course, the notion of misperceptions and misinformation presupposes knowledge of what is real and accurate. The problem is that, as we have seen, experts disagree, which then means that the mainstream media are burdened with determining what is to count as correct opinion, a task which they are clearly incompetent to undertake.[144] Neither Meek nor Bridgman considered this problem.

We can draw a few preliminary conclusions from this discussion of the utterances of the moral entrepreneurs whom we call experts and from the pushback their utterances generated from others, equally expert. There is a concept in game theory called "cheap talk."[145] It is defined as "communication between players that does not directly affect the payoffs of the game," and exists when persons with different capabilities or expertise send the same message. Both incapable and capable individuals looking for a job, for example, will tell a prospective employer they are capable even if they are not. Michael Spence, a 2001 Nobel Laureate in economics, argued in a classical study several years ago that one solution to the problem of cheap talk is educational credentialing.[146] Because it is

---

[143] Debora Van Brenk, "Researcher, Expert Combats Conspiracies with Facts," *Western News*, (May 6, 2020).

[144] See Bridgman et al., "The Causes and Consequences of the COVID-19 Misperceptions: Understanding the Role of News and Social Media," *Harvard Kennedy School (HKS) Misinformation Review*, 1, (June 18, 2020); see also "New Carleton Study Finds COVID-19 Conspiracies and Misinformation Spreading Online," Carleton University News Release, (May 20, 2020); Philip Ball and Amy Maxman, "The Epic Battle against Misinformation and Conspiracy Theories," *Nature*, 581 (2020): 371–74; Julian Kestler-D'Amours, "COVID-19 Conspiracy Theories a 'Public Health Crisis' in Canada, Experts Say," CBC News, (August 4, 2020).

[145] James R. Rogers, "Cheap Talk and Expertise," *Law and Liberty*, (August 18, 2020).

[146] Michael Spence, "Job Market Signaling," *Quarterly Journal of Economics*, 87 (1973): 355–74.

easier or cheaper for high-capability individuals to invest in credentialing or education, they will. So, observing whether a person claiming to be highly capable is credentialed gives the prospective employer additional information about whether he or she is as highly capable as they claim.

The same logic applies to alleged experts. Invariably, they claim to know what they are talking about, but by and large we only trust credentialed experts. That means, most of the time, and with respect to the pandemic, somebody with a PhD or an M.D., preferably from an elite school. Such a solution to this well-known game-theoretic problem, however, as Rogers pointed out, leads to a "secondary cheap-talk problem," namely that a credentialed expert might opine on matters outside his or her expertise or on matters that do not admit of expert answers. That is, there remains the problem of "the possibility of overreach of experts as a group."[147] So why do experts speak outside areas of their expertise and thus invite public skepticism? First, experts often think it is more persuasive to present issues in either/or terms in order to get what they think is the proper policy response. Science, with all its nuances and qualifications, is too subtle for the public to grasp, say the experts, because the public is not comprised of experts. Thus, Health Canada officials opposed self-testing for COVID-19 because "without the guidance of a health-care professional, there is a significant risk that a patient could use the home test kit improperly or misinterpret the results." As Marni Soupcoff commented: "Health Canada thinks we're incompetent idiots" (*National Post*, September 4, 2020). Of course, the problem of simplification is exacerbated by the practices of contemporary journalists. Second, especially with policy debates, experts understandably seek to take advantage of their status and extend their authority by expressing their preferences as if it were simply a matter of expertise. This essentially economic argument has nothing in common, so to speak, with Foucault's power-knowledge perspective. The effect, however, is to reinforce Foucault's insight and explain why the media report the unsubstantiated opinions of credentialed medical experts on matters about which they have no expertise.

---

[147] Consider the argument of David Rothman, "Why Tech Didn't Save Us from COVID-19," *MIT Technology Review*, (July 2020), particularly as concerns administrative technologies and the "sclerotic bureaucracy" at the U.S. Centers for Disease Control. His argument could be applied to Canada with minimal changes.

Comparisons between
Sweden and Canada

Several countries around the world chose to respond to the COVID-19 pandemic threat other than by using the suppressive approach of national lockdowns, either by ignoring the threat altogether or by adopting complex strategies to mitigate it. At the opposite end of Chinese-style suppression, some chose to do nothing, and were widely criticized as being irresponsible. This happened in Nicaragua, the small Central American country ruled by Sandinista dictator Daniel Ortega. Worse than delaying and not adopting any initial protective measures, the Sandinista regime actively organized mass political rallies and government party celebrations across the country, ignoring the rampant propagation and the rising death toll.[148]

In Belarus, which is also ruled by a dictator, Alexander Lukashenko, the government did almost nothing to combat COVID-19. Lukashenko called it "the flu" and made fun of the moral panic in Europe and in North America, calling it "corona psychosis." He also spurned the WHO's help (and loans to pay for it). As Brian Giesbrecht put it: "Belarus just muddled through."[149] The result was not streets filled with corpses, but "a decidedly moderate death count." The gross comparative data, in short, are decidedly mixed. Lockdowns vary in intensity, depending on the jurisdiction, but typically are restrictive of people's actions, movements, and as we saw, of the ability of many to earn a living and care for their families. In Alberta, for example, where the rules where somewhat more relaxed than in Quebec, Kenney ordered all non-essential businesses to close. Liquor stores, pharmacies, and grocery stores were permitted to remain open.

---

[148] Alfonso Flores Bermúdez and Frances Robles, "Resisting Lockdown, Nicaragua Becomes a Place of Midnight Burials," *New York Times*, (May 31, 2020).
[149] Brian Giesbrecht, "Rejecting 'Corona Psychosis' Could be Good For our Health," *C2C*, (September 10, 2020).

Restaurants could not offer in-restaurant dining but could deliver or offer pickup. The closures included close-contact personal services such as tattoo parlours, salons, and barber shops; non-essential health services such as dentistry, physiotherapy, and massage; and retail businesses such as clothing and electronics stores. Retail stores were permitted to continue operating online and offer curbside pickup. Mostly, small businesses bore the brunt of the lockdown. Municipalities followed suit and closed playgrounds, parks, and outdoor recreational areas. In between comprehensive lockdowns and the apparently catastrophic Sandinista approach there are several gradations, the most notorious of which (Belarus aside) has been the Swedish approach.

Media world-wide and governments in countries adopting lockdowns have widely maligned Sweden's mitigating strategy.[150] Some hold it up as a model of what never to do. Others are promoting the false notion that Sweden has irresponsibly chosen not to protect its citizens at all. For all the acceptance of the mitigating strategy in Sweden itself, support is not unanimous. A group of Swedish academics urged the world not to adopt the Swedish model, calling it callous in its alleged disregard for life. These concerned scholars cited authorities from the WHO condemning herd immunity as a strategy. "It can lead to a very brutal arithmetic that does not put people and life and [relief from] suffering at the center of that

---

[150] Nick Cohen, "Sweden's Covid-19 Policy is a Model for the Right. It's Also a Deadly Folly," *Guardian*, (May 23, 2020); Thomas Erdbrink, "Sweden Tries Out a New Status: Pariah State," *New York Times*, (June 22, 2020); Peter S. Goodman, "Sweden Has Become the World's Cautionary Tale," *New York Times*, (July 7, 2020). Goodman's damning NYT article is ironic considering that New York State and New York City in particular have one of the worst COVID-19 records of any jurisdiction in the world; Christina Farr, "Sweden Kept its Country Relatively Open during the Coronavirus Pandemic, But its Elderly Paid a Price," CNBC, (July 17, 2020); Maddy Savage, "What's Going Wrong in Sweden's Care Homes,?" BBC News (Stockholm), (May 19, 2020); David Keyton, "Sweden Could Have Handled Coronavirus Response Better, Chief Epidemiologist Admits," Global News, (June 3, 2020); Michael Birnbaum, "Scientist behind Sweden's Covid-19 Strategy Suggests It Allowed Too Many Deaths," *Washington Post*, (June 4, 2020); and Sharon Begley and Andrew Joseph, "The U.S. is the Accidental Sweden, which Could Make the Fall 'Catastrophic' for Covid-19," *Statnews*, (July 15, 2020). Even though some have accused Sweden of being Donald Trump-like in its strategy for COVID-19, by which they mean careless and callous, Trump has also attacked Sweden for not locking down. See Morten Buttler and Nick Rigillo, "Trump's Latest Attack on Sweden Revives Covid-19 Controversy," Bloomberg, (May 1, 2020).

equation," said Mike Ryan, executive director of WHO's Health Emergencies Program.[151]

Others have praised Sweden as a great triumph of a responsible and libertarian approach. What seems clear, even in the thick fog of accusation, is that praise for and attacks against Sweden's strategy took place within ideological battles at the heart of political and scientific circles precisely because Sweden's approach could make fools out of many politicians and scientists by calling into question their panic and moral entrepreneurialism. In previous sections, we have drawn attention to examples of bureaucratic mission creep and highly questionable instances of bureaucratic overreach, but our purpose was not so much to criticize as to understand a complex social and political phenomenon. Now, considering Sweden, we intend to offer neither vindication nor condemnation. We attempt to look at events, decisions, and approaches outside such ideological bubbles.

There are many reasons to look closely at Sweden's experiment. Lockdowns and mitigating strategies dealing with pandemics are all policy experiments. Given that Sweden has from the start adopted an independent mitigating strategy and has not fundamentally changed course, it presents a rare contrarian case from within a developed and democratic nation. Sweden's policies have remained consistent and its data gathering and reporting practices are credible. The Swedish case can be used to contrast and evaluate strategies used elsewhere, especially as compared to suppression strategies other countries adopted.

Media coverage and some policy and scientific advocates have portrayed the lockdowns as "conventional," which implied that anything short of a full lockdown was illegitimate. In our view, this was just another expression of moral panic. Something is usually called conventional when it has become a habitual and commonly recognized practice. But there had never been full lockdowns of entire countries before, let alone a cascade of them. There is nothing conventional about the 2020 lockdown. Rather, as noted, the genuine conventional practice has been to quarantine the infected, not the healthy and sick alike. Both the suppressive and the mitigating strategies are experiments, despite the widespread agreement regarding lockdowns. Our view that both approaches are experiments is neither idiosyncratic nor novel. Camilla Stoltenberg, director-general of

---

[151] Sigurd Bergmann et al., "Sweden Hoped Herd Immunity Would Curb COVID-19. Don't Do What We Did. It's Not Working," *USA Today*, (July 21, 2020). Curiously, within a few weeks, however, Ryan was praising the Swedish model.

the Norwegian Institute of Public Health, for example, expressed the situation in precisely these terms: "We may regard both the Swedish [mitigating] and the Norwegian [suppressive] approaches as experiments," she said, and went on to point out what would then be an obvious extension of that understanding. Because they are both experiments, still unfolding as we write, and will continue to unfold some for some time to come, "we will know only in a couple of years which strategy worked best."[152] In short, the jury charged with deciding the success or failure of these alternative strategies is still out.

Sweden's response, which also claimed to be in accordance with science, presented an opportunity to examine the effectiveness of approaches used elsewhere and the underlying reasons and claims of others, their decision-making and organizational structures, their policies for national emergencies and health security, as well as for economic and social policy, and their overall response to crisis. Sweden may not be a perfect model, and we do not mean to imply that the Swedish way is beyond reproach, but we recognize that comparisons have the potential to show what others have done wrong or have done right.

From the start, the objective of Sweden's strategy as a key element of national defence has been the comprehensive protection of the Swedish national community. That meant: (1) protecting at-risk groups, mostly the elderly; (2) keeping schools open; (3) keeping the economy open; and (4) avoiding a health-care collapse.[153] In other words, much more than medical priorities and the desire to save lives has been on the table. Their goal has never been to stop the virus from spreading, nor has it been to eradicate it. Rather, the Swedish strategy rests on the epidemiological assumption that one cannot stop the propagation of a virus by closing down entire societies. As Anders Tegnell, Sweden's state epidemiologist, said, "I don't think that this is a disease we can eradicate." Not now and maybe not with a vaccine: "If you look at comparable diseases like the flu and other respiratory viruses, we are not even close to eradicating them despite the fact that we have a vaccine. I personally believe that this is a disease we are going to have to learn to live with." He explained that suppression may work for a while in places like New Zealand and Iceland, "but with the

---

[152] Michael Birnbaum, "Scientist behind Sweden's Covid-19 Strategy Suggests It Allowed Too Many Deaths."
[153] Swedish Armed Forces, "Totalförsvaret," https://www.forsvarsmakten.se/sv/om-forsvarsmakten/totalforsvaret/.

global world we have today, keeping a disease like this away has never been possible in the past and it would be even more surprising if it were possible in the future."[154] In short, the Swedish objective was to slow down the infection rate and to mitigate as much as possible the effects of the virus upon the medical system and Swedish society. To achieve that effect, Sweden activated its long-standing "Totalförsvaret" (Total Defence) strategy.[155]

The comprehensiveness of the approach was already built into this emergency strategy: "The goal of military defense is to defend Sweden individually and together with others, within and outside the country, and promote our security. The goal of civil defense is threefold: protect civilian population, ensure the most important societal functions and contribute to the Armed Forces' ability in the event of an armed attack." One can best understand Sweden's response to the COVID-19 crisis in the context of executing a comprehensive military and civil defence strategy. The activation of the first two elements of the civil defence, (absent the support of the Swedish Forces since there was no armed attack), has constituted the core of Swedish action.

The Swedish government's Total Defence security strategy was devised during the Cold War, when it was designed to protect Sweden's neutrality from possible Soviet attacks. The strategy was deemed obsolete in the optimistic mood that followed the collapse of the Soviet Union. But in a jolt of realpolitik, a revamped Swedish defence bill brought it back in 2015 following the 2014 Russian invasion of Crimea. By the spring of 2018, the defence commission chaired by Björn von Sydow sent an updated brochure to every household in Sweden outlining the core of the country's emergency preparedness in case of a foreign invasion. The document did not mention Russia by name and the strategy had been modernized to include other threats such as natural disasters, sabotage, disinformation, and cyber-attacks.[156]

---

[154] Freddie Sayers, "Why We Aren't Wearing Masks in Sweden," interview with Anders Tegnell, (July 24, 2020).

[155] Swedish Armed Forces, "Totalförsvaret." To our knowledge, the first source to make the connection between the COVID-19 strategy and Total Defence is Elisabeth Braw, "What Sweden Can Teach Us about Coronavirus," *Politico*, (July 3, 2020).

[156] Björn von Sydow, "Resilience: Planning for Sweden's 'Total Defence,'" *NATO Review*, (April 4, 2018). The news about Total Defence in Sweden was covered at

Starting with the first version, Total Defence in the military mobilization of Swedish society contemplated the participation and involvement of basic institutions, local authorities, hospitals, private enterprise, and volunteer individuals in the protection of the realm. It was not conceived as something to be applied to or imposed on a passive population. The strategy, European observers at the Warsaw Institute remarked, "reinforces the individual's independence from the state's support in case of crisis: every Swedish citizen should be able to manage without the support of public institutions" for several days.[157] The emergency mobilization of Swedish assets and individual participation in such enterprise had been fresh in the minds of Swedes for some time prior to the outbreak.

In 2017, a defence commission was appointed to fine-tune the strategic direction for a new defence bill. It resulted in the December 2017 report, "Resilience: The Total Defence Concept and the Development of Civil Defence 2021-2025." The document emphasized that Sweden "needs to prepare systematically and comprehensively for the worst-case scenario of war."[158] Beyond physical survival, the document included the defence of the "open society and the rule of law." Crucial to the COVID-19 response, it also included preparations to transition health-care operations so as to be capable of accommodating tens of thousands of casualties.[159]

The same commission emphasized that "the Swedish population needs to perform basic economic transactions during war." Accordingly, "Sweden has the basic legal requirements to manage either a hybrid situation [of emergency] or a war," which essentially meant that there was no need to reorganize state power in the event of a military or civil emergency. This approach emphasized the primacy of economy to

---

the time by CBC in Canada. See Nahlah Ayed, "Sweden Calls on Citizens to Prepare for War, Terror Attacks – and Fake News," CBC News, (May 31, 2018). The CBC report emphasized how Sweden would deal with the disinformational aspect of "fake news."

[157] Warsaw Institute, "The Swedish 'Total Defence,'" (June 15, 2018). WarsawInstitute.org

[158] An online summary of the document on the Swedish government website speaks of protecting "security, freedom and autonomy." See Swedish Defence Commission, "Resilience" (Summary), n.p., n.d. https://www.government.se/4afeb9/globalassets/government/dokument/forsvarsdepa rtementet/resilience---report-summary---20171220ny.pdf.

[159] Björn von Sydow, "Resilience: Planning for Sweden's "Total Defence."

national life, absolved the government from having to formulate emergency measures anew, and removed the temptation to use crises as a means to improve or advance the political fortunes of those in power, as has happened in Canada. Even so, in Sweden the party in power has been accused of seeking to augment its power during the crisis.

Crisis situations activate a command structure that leads from local authorities all the way to the central government in Stockholm. Its civilian authority flows from the Ministry of Justice but in any Swedish emergency or crisis, even though Sweden is a unitary state, no single government organ has the exclusive responsibility for all areas of the country. The Swedish Civil Contingencies Agency (CCA) is responsible for issues concerning civil protection, public safety, emergency management, and civil defence in the absence of war, so long as no military authority has responsibility. The CCA involves governmental authorities, regional authorities, municipalities, experts, academics, private enterprises, and business communities, and has "the same resources and modus operandi regardless of social disruption."[160]

Emergency management rests on widely accepted principles in Swedish society of proximity, equality, and responsibility. Proximity is akin to the principle of subsidiarity, the notion that problems are best solved by the decisions of those closest and most affected by them. Equality means that the organizing of operations, as much as possible, remains the same as under non-emergency conditions, and responsibility means that those charged with operations under normal conditions continue in authority. In the language used above, these principles act as a buffer against the panic-driven, practical inexperience of outside experts among those seeking to assert their power-knowledge. While it does not exclude experts, it does keep the common sense of local authorities in the mix on the ground.[161] Having a comprehensive plan fresh in citizens' minds enabled the authorities to focus on the practical task at hand; namely, the peculiarities to the COVID-19 crisis and how to apply existing plans to it. They could also consider the problem of how to tackle the crisis and move beyond it

---

[160] Swedish Civil Contingencies Agency, "What Does the MSB Do?" https://www.msb.se/en/operations/ongoing-operations/coronavirus---covid-19/what-does-msb-do/.

[161] For more on the structures of Swedish authority in case of emergencies, see European Commission, "Vademecum – Civil Protection, Country Profile, Sweden," https://ec.europa.eu/echo/files/civil_protection/vademecum/se/2-se-1.html.

rather than simply react to the immediate point of the spear and attempt to manage public relation strategies in order to persuade the electorate of the wisdom of government choices that had already been made.

Quite deliberately, therefore, the structures and organization of emergency response in Sweden reflected a broader attitude toward unforeseen situations. It is clear this approach went a long way beyond the strict protection of life: "Community protection and preparedness are about ensuring that the whole of society can cope with both minor and major accidents and crises. Emergency preparedness is intended to protect the lives and health of the population, society's ability to function, and the capacity to uphold basic values such as democracy, the rule of law, and human rights."[162] The result of this process has been to foster a well-prepared population, a society aware of a plan of action and of the structures set into place to deal with a comprehensive emergency, including threats to public health. Preparations for emergencies go a long way to defuse anxiety and tame the temptations of panic in the absence of knowing what to do and when. It also prepared people to trust the process that the government had set in place with popular support, allowed people to act responsibly and independently when needed, protected their rights, and helped ensure an awareness of media hype and "fake news." The Swedes, in short, also prepared for a moral panic and were thus able to avoid one.

Sweden's government is currently formed by Stefan Löfven's Social Democrat (Sweden's equivalent to Canada's NDP) minority coalition. The Swedish government never seems to have considered the Chinese lockdown model as a guide, or what Swedish academics called the "lockdown consensus." At the outset of the COVID-19 crisis, Sweden's "light touch" attempted to limit the spread of the virus while simultaneously mitigating its economic and social impacts. It included the protection of people's lives, concentrating on the vulnerable, and ensured that the country's health-care capacity remained uncompromised.

In addition to limiting the spread of the virus and ensuring the integrity of health-care resources, Sweden has tried to limit the virus's impact on critical services, on people, and on businesses. It supplied appropriate information to citizens so that they could protect themselves and provided

---

[162] Government of Sweden, "Emergency Preparedness," https://www.government.se/government-policy/emergency-preparedness/.

effective co-ordination of a range of measures implemented across the country. Under the "light touch," Sweden's main recommendations for achieving these objectives included such obvious hygienic practices as frequent hand-washing, maintaining physical distance from others, working from home when possible, avoiding large social gatherings, being cautious when visiting the elderly and individuals in at-risk groups, staying home if exhibiting COVID-19 symptoms, and urging those above age 70 to limit contacts and avoid large gatherings. Visits to retirement homes were not initially banned but the rising death rate among seniors in long-term care facilities led the Swedish government to tighten the rules. In addition, an investigation has been launched to determine whether there has been criminal intent connected with the administration of retirement homes and long-term care facilities.[163]

Universities and high schools were ordered closed, but elementary and middle schools remained open. Borders remained open but some restrictions for travelers from specific countries were later put into place to satisfy the European Union.[164] Distancing guidelines for shops, bars, restaurants, malls, markets, and general businesses remained voluntary and these establishments remained open in an effort to protect people's livelihoods and the national economy. Most Swedes stayed home and many businesses opted to close their doors because of the reduced business traffic, but such actions were not as a result of state orders. In any event, Swedish law was limited in the degree to which it could order lockdowns or prohibit citizens from going to the beach. That is, under Swedish law, an enforced lockdown was not a realistic option in the absence of overwhelming threats.[165] Moreover, the Public Health Agency thought that voluntary measures would work as well as compulsory ones, not because Swedes are inherently more responsible than other peoples

---

[163] Niclas Rolander, "Sweden Starts Criminal Probe into Care Home after Coronavirus Deaths," Bloomberg, (May 8, 2020).

[164] Government of Sweden, "Official Information on the Covid-19 Pandemic." https://www.krisinformation.se/en/hazards-and-risks/disasters-and-incidents/2020/official-information-on-the-new-coronavirus.

[165] Ross Clark, "Is This the Real Reason Sweden Didn't Lock Down?" *Spectator USA*, (June 11, 2020). In late September, Anders Tegnell indicated that, if necessary, Sweden may introduce local and short-term restrictions on the size of public gatherings, *National Post*, (September 24, 2020).

but because, by having government authorities tell Swedes they were responsible, they acted that way.[166]

Swedish medical officials also explained that there was no evidence to sustain the claim that fully enforced lockdowns were effective measures against viruses.[167] As we have noted earlier, Canada's minister of Health and the chief medical officer voiced similar opinions in the early days following the declaration of a pandemic. The difference between Canada and Sweden in this respect was that the decisions of Swedish authorities were supported by a well-thought-out strategy. That is, decision-makers in Sweden were also concerned with the consequences of lockdowns and their side effects. Tegnell observed: "In the same way that all drugs have side effects, measures against a pandemic also have negative effects." He also pointed out that part of the mandate of his national office was to consider a wider "spectrum of public health" than was constituted by the virus alone.[168] Tegnell took a sufficiently broad view of public health that he could consider, for instance, the dire effects on people's overall health caused by massive unemployment. "Unemployed people are a great threat to public health," he told the *Daily Mail*.[169] Because Swedish officials did not seek to stop or eradicate the virus, they chose to embrace a long-term strategy that is more consistent with epidemiological reality and established scientific knowledge, as well as being in accord with the principles outlined in the national emergency plans and the simple expectations of life in a constitutional democracy.

Concern for the unintended consequences of a lockdown raised additional questions regarding the usefulness of that option. Imposing a full lockdown without concern about how to end it presented enormous risks, especially when one cannot know how long it would last, whether

---

[166] Rachel Irwin, "The Truth about Sweden's Voluntary Lockdown," *Spectator*, (September 22, 2020).

[167] Johan Giesecke, former chief medical officer of Sweden in an interview with *UnHerd*, "Why Lockdowns are the Wrong Policy – Swedish Expert Prof. Johan Giesecke," (April 17, 2020), https://youtu.be/bfN2JWifLCY; see also John Fund and Joel Hay, "Has Sweden Found the Right Solution to the Coronavirus?" *National Review*, (April 6, 2020).

[168] Love Liman and Niclas Rolander, "Swedish COVID Expert Says the World Still Doesn't Understand," *National Post*, (June 30, 2020).

[169] Ian Gallagher, "Scientist Leading Sweden's Battle against Coronavirus Says Britain's Lockdown Has Gone Too Far as His Country Allows Bars, Restaurants and Schools to Remain Open," *Daily Mail*, (April 5, 2020).

weeks or months, or even longer, depending on what the changing targets would be. The Swedes knew well enough, however, that a lockdown of a magnitude and duration sufficient to try to eliminate the propagation of a virus would not be sustainable in a liberal democratic society in the same way that it could be imposed by an authoritarian state like the People's Republic of China.[170] Tegnell and the Swedish leadership of medical professionals were sufficiently educated in the liberal arts to understand prudence as well as medical knowledge and quickly grasped the key theoretical and practical political and economic issues involved. Tegnell, for example, has been a member of the Royal Swedish Academy of War Sciences since 2005. Our Canadian equivalents have manifested no such broad understanding of political and economic reality. As we have seen, Tam, for instance, advocated the full containment and the curtailment of liberties among potentially infected citizens with a clinical matter-of-factness that showed no thought of the implications that such actions have for our social and political traditions. This does not mean that Tam does not possess such knowledge, but if she does, it has been neither publicly displayed nor deployed in Canada.

Tegnell worried that in the process of instituting a tight lockdown, one would have to impose a wide variety of draconian measures, using legal means that would then be imposed through the use of police force that would violate the letter and spirit of liberty and damage the fabric of an open society. Johan Giesecke, one of Tegnell's predecessors as state epidemiologist (1995-2005), expressed similar concerns. Giesecke spent 2005 to 2014 as the first chief scientist of the European Centre for Disease Prevention and Control (ECDC).[171] Early in September 2020, he was given a senior advisory position as vice-chair of the Strategic and Technical Advisory Group on Infectious Hazards (STAG-IH) at the WHO, advising the director-general on responses to the pandemic.[172] Like Tegnell, Giesecke also worried that the maintenance of order and the rule of law would be impaired by an angry and frustrated citizenry legitimately reacting

---

[170] Elisabeth Braw, "What Sweden Can Teach Us about Coronavirus."

[171] World Health Organization, "Giesecke, Johan is Member of the Strategic and Technical Advisory Group for Infectious Hazards (STAG-IH)." Vaccine specialist Gary Kobinger at the Infectious Disease Research Centre at Université Laval is the only Canadian among the 13-member advisory panel.

[172] Hannah Osborne, "Sweden's 'Herd Immunity' Mastermind Gets Promoted by WHO," *Newsweek,* (September 2, 2020).

to being forcibly confined. They were concerned about the potential for escalation of civil disobedience.

In addition, Swedish authorities were aware that a lockdown would lead to adverse health consequences resulting from postponing crucial services, the detrimental mental health consequences of closing business and depriving people of their jobs, and a host of consequences leading to alcoholism, drug abuse, family violence, child abuse, depression, and suicide, all of which we discussed above. As Scott Young wrote in a piece for *Maclean's* discussing the Swedish strategy, the Swedes "are simply betting that a long-term voluntary mitigation strategy will yield better public health outcomes than a short-term coercive containment one."[173] He is correct about Swedish expectations of better public health outcomes, but it was not really a bet so much as a carefully conceived strategy. It would be more accurate to say that countries other than Sweden placed a bet, though many of them did not know it.

For example, there is no evidence that health authorities in Canada were aware of the unintended effects of their decisions. If they had such an awareness, they do not appear to have initiated strategies to mitigate the ill effects in any way. As mentioned in section 4, there are continuing reports, for example, of a significant increase in the number of deaths by drug overdoses. Consider the following data: in August, an updated report on B.C. showed that the upward trend of drug-overdose deaths related to the COVID-19 crisis continued for three consecutive months. The report showed a high incidence among Indigenous people disproportionate to their demographic profile. The B.C. number of COVID-19 deaths between March and July was reported at 195 while the number of total deaths by overdose in the same five-month period is 758, nearly four times the number of COVID-19 deaths. Worse, the number of reported deaths by COVID-19 peaked inside this period in April at 87 and dropped to 11 and 19 for June and July, respectively. The number of deaths from drug overdoses in those same two months was 177 and 175, respectively. The average number of deaths from drugs in the province for January and February 2020, pre-COVID-19 lockdown, was 76.5. That is, in the three months of June, July, and August, there has been a monthly excess of 100 people dead as an indirect consequence of the lockdown.

---

[173] Scott Young, "Lessons from Kronavirus: Is Sweden's Anti-lockdown Approach More Strategic than it Seems?" *Maclean's*, (May 12, 2020).

In September, statistics from Alberta reveal the same correlation between the lockdown and a sharp increase in the number of deaths by drug overdose. Drug deaths more than doubled in the second quarter of 2020 in Alberta, jumping to 301 from 148 in the first quarter. Overall, the increase constitutes a 28 percent spike compared to the first six months of 2019.[174] As was the case in British Columbia, more Albertans have died of drug overdoses than from COVID-19. The Quebec coroner's office has detected similar trends in that province for the early summer months of 2020.[175] Preliminary reports show a similar pattern across the country. In early August 2020, prior to the release of Alberta's data, Tam issued a statement. "Tragically, in many regions of the country, the COVID-19 pandemic is contributing to an increase in drug-related overdoses and deaths," she said, implying that the illness induces people to such actions and not the policies resulting from the lockdown. After addressing the B.C. statistics briefly, she went on to say: "Yukon reported twice as many overdose deaths in the first half of 2020 when compared with the same period in 2019. Saskatchewan is reporting historic levels of overdoses and overdose deaths, and in Quebec, July saw the highest number of overdose deaths in Montreal in over five years."[176] Henry openly acknowledged the relationship between drug abuse and the lockdown conditions in her province: "It's dismaying to know that all of the work that we have done around responding to COVID-19 has been a contributing factor to the numbers of deaths that we're seeing from the toxic drug supply here in British Columbia and across Canada."[177] Dismaying? This single unintended consequence has produced more dead in Canada than the disease and the provincial health officer admits to being dismayed at the results of her own policies. Did she even consider changing them? Not a chance.

The toll on mental health, while not yet fully quantified, is equally significant. Nova Scotia has reported a 35 percent increase in calls seeking

[174] Jason Herring, "Opioid Deaths More than Double in Alberta during COVID-19 Pandemic," *Calgary Sun*, (September 23, 2020).

[175] See Jennifer Yoon, "Quebec Coroner's Office Warns about Unusually High Number of Drug-Related Deaths," CBC News, (August 6, 2020).

[176] Theresa Tam, "Statement from the Chief Public Health Officer of Canada," Public Health Agency of Canada, (August 26, 2020).

[177] Quoted in Rhianna Schmunk, "B.C. Marks 3rd Straight Month with More than 170 Overdose Deaths," CBC News, (August 25, 202).

help from the mental health hotline as compared to 2019.[178] A recent review authored by Samantha K. Brooks of King's College, London, and a group of colleagues, looked at the existing literature on the psychological effects of quarantines. Brooks is an expert on the psychological impact of disaster situations, is a member of the Health Protection Research Unit at King's and works on the Group Responses After Disasters & Emergencies (GRADE) study. Most of the papers the review examined report negative psychological effects that include post-traumatic stress syndrome, confusion, anger, and anxiety, for instance. Many researchers have suggested that these outcomes will have long-lasting effects.[179]

Experts, advocates, and researchers from various universities, agencies, and organizations have been sounding alarms about the risks of increased domestic violence under lockdown conditions. In particular, warnings regarding violence against women were voiced earlier as a consequence of the most suppressive of all COVID-19 lockdowns, that of China. As early as March 7, less than a week before the WHO declared a pandemic, Bethany Allen-Ebrahimian called attention to the rise of domestic violence against women during the lockdown in China: "The number of domestic violence incidents reported to a nearby Jingzhou police station had tripled in February, compared to the same period the previous year."[180] The WHO issued more comprehensive warnings about the risks and dangers before the end of March.[181] In early April 2020, Kelsey Hegarty and Laura Tarzia of the Faculty of Medicine at the University of Melbourne drew attention to the effects of trapping women in violent situations at home as a result of COVID-19 quarantine and isolation requirements, compounded by unemployment, financial stress, crowding, and so on.[182] Mark Townsend at the *Guardian* reported a spike in Britain, where Refuge, the largest domestic-abuse charity in the country, registered a 25 percent increase in

---

[178] Michael Lightstone, "Mental-health Crisis Line Sees Surge in Calls due to Pandemic," *Halifax Today*, (August 11, 2020).

[179] Samantha K. Brooks et al., "The Psychological Impact of Quarantines and How to Reduce It: Rapid Review of Evidence," *Lancet*, vol. 395: 10227, (March 14, 2020).

[180] Bethany Allen-Ebrahimian, "China's Domestic Violence Epidemic," *Axios*, (March 7, 2020).

[181] WHO, "COVID-19 and Violence against Women," (March 26, 2020).

[182] Kelsey Hegarty and Laura Tarzia, "Domestic Violence, Isolation and COVID-19," *Pursuit*, University of Melbourne, (April 7, 2020).

calls for help in the first two weeks of the lockdown.[183] Reports from around the world recorded the same trend. Researchers Caroline Beltinger-Lopez and Alexandra Bro traced the trends directly connecting the COVID-19 restriction to the increased risks in domestic violence. They reported increases in Mexico, Brazil, Australia, France, Germany, South Africa, and the United States. They noted that the number of calls for help had dropped in Chile and Bolivia, likely resulting from the same violent conditions at home preventing women from contacting outside resources.[184] In early April, Amanda Taub of the New York Times captured the massive failure of governments that locked down, to protect women and children. Noting that the evidence pointed toward domestic violence incidents becoming "more frequent, more severe, and more dangerous," Taub didn't mince words. "Governments largely failed to prepare for the way the new [COVID-19] public health measures would create opportunities for abusers to terrorize their victims. Now, many are scrambling to offer services to those at risk," she wrote.[185] Just three days earlier, Adrian Humphreys raised the question in Canada in the context of changes in crime patterns caused by the lockdown. He noted, for example, that domestic violence had reportedly grown by 62 percent in Edmonton.[186]

Taub's observations fit Canada like a glove. Toronto-based lawyer, women's advocate, and commentator Kathryn Marshall has observed the rise of violence against women related to COVID-19 in Canada.[187] At the end of April, nearly six weeks after the start of the lockdown in Canada, the federal minister for Women and Gender Equality, Maryam Monsef, spoke out about the link between the lockdown and the creation of "powder keg" conditions enabling domestic violence to rise by as much as

---

[183] Mark Townsend, "Revealed: Surge in Domestic Violence during COVID-19 Crisis," *Guardian*, (April 12, 2020).

[184] Caroline Beltinger-Lopez and Alexandra Bro, "A Double Pandemic: Domestic Violence in the Age of COVID-19," Council of Foreign Relations, (May 13, 2020); see also Kirsty Johnston, "Covid19 Coronavirus: Domestic Violence is the Second, Silent Epidemic Amid Lockdown," *New Zealand Herald*, (April 12, 2020).

[185] Amanda Taub, "A New COVID-19 Crisis: Domestic Abuses Rise Worldwide," *New York Times*, (April 6, 2020).

[186] Adrian Humphreys, "Crime in a Time of COVID-19: How the Pandemic is Changing Criminality in our Neighborhoods," *National Post*, (April 3, 2020).

[187] Kathryn Marshall, "The Pandemic's Epidemic of Violence against Women," *National Post*, (October 8, 2020).

30 percent. Monsef claimed then that calls for help had increased "by some 400 percent."[188] The claims also came with the realization that many women were unable to seek help while in COVID-19 mandated isolation. The implication was that the numbers may even be higher than those the minister cited. Moreover, sending $50 million extra to shelters and advocacy organizations might not significantly reduce the amount of abuse under lockdown conditions, not least because the announcements of extra money came during the lockdown. Post-facto funding could not solve the problem that government policy caused, even while the prime minister almost scolded people to stay home to save lives, largely creating the conditions that increased the risks of violence in many families. No journalist, to our knowledge, has asked Monsef if she raised these known risks of "empowering abusers" of women and children while the government considered COVID-19 lockdown strategies.

Typically, COVID-19 does not medically affect children. They may contract the virus, carry it, and in some cases transmit it, but few in the millions who have been infected have gotten seriously sick, and there has only been one known child death in Canada from the virus. A new report co-published and authored by teams from the Alberta Children's Hospital Research Institute, the O'Brien Institute for Public Health at the University of Calgary, and Children First Canada, a child advocacy organization, shed light on the unintended effects of the COVID-19 lockdowns, focusing specifically on children. The report is entitled "Raising Canada 2020."[189] It called attention to a series of indicators that showed how children's quality of life has measurably deteriorated during the COVID-19 lockdown regime. These included an increase in poverty cases, with 29 percent of Canadians reporting having experienced moderate to major difficulties meeting their financial obligations. A 95 percent reduction in physical activity among children aged four to 11 and over 99 percent among youth aged 12 to 17 has had bad effects. Families have experienced difficulties finding childcare, especially for children with disabilities. There have been setbacks in learning, driven by school closures, lack of access to online resources, and stresses about online

---

[188] See Raisa Patel, "Minister Says COVID-19 is Empowering Domestic Violence Abusers as Rates Increase in Parts of Canada," CBC News, (April 27, 2020).
[189] Gail MacKean et al., "Raising Canada 2020," Children First Canada, 2020. https://childrenfirstcanada.org/raising-canada.

learning. There is a lack of access to timely health care, especially for those with chronic conditions or complex disabilities, delays in assessments, therapies, and surgeries, and a likely increase in sexual, physical, and emotional abuse. The report noted that the main source of death now among children ages 10 to 14 is suicide. A recent UNICEF publication, *Global Status Report Preventing Violence against Children*, anticipated that "the economic devastation wrought by COVID-19 and the response to it may take years to overcome, and could exacerbate economic inequalities, poverty, unemployment, and household financial insecurity. These long-term effects can be expected to drive homicides and violent assault back at least to their pre-lockdown levels and could potentially impact many risk factors for later violence, including brain development, early learning, and schooling."[190]

Some evidence of the rise of various dangers for children during the lockdowns has been trickling in as lockdowns continue, but it will be some time before there can be a comprehensive examination of these consequences. In April, the Internet Child Exploitation (ICE) unit of the Alberta Law Enforcement Response Team (ALERT) alerted the public to a rise in online child exploitation activity for March. ICE investigates child pornography cases, computer-related child sexual abuse, internet child luring, voyeurism involving minors, and child sex trade/tourism. The "unit's two-year average of 110 cases" a month for March 2020 jumped to 243, more than double, and considering that schools were closed for only half of March, the expectation was for a higher number for April.[191] With the school closures and the delivery of instruction switching to online platforms, more children were online for longer periods, and more people were off work and staying home trolling the internet, creating near-optimal conditions for online sexual predators. By June, ALERT felt more comfortable in making the connection of an increase in cases and in the number of related arrests around the province to the COVID-19 lockdown.[192] Similar increases have been reported all over the country. By

---

[190] UNICEF, *Global Status Report Preventing Violence against Children*, (Geneva: World Health Organization, 2020: xi).

[191] Demi Knight, "ICE Reports Spike in Online Child Exploitation Cases in Alberta amid COVID-19 Pandemic," Global News (Alberta), (April 21, 2020).

[192] See Melissa Gilligan, "Spike in Online Child Exploitation Reports in Alberta 'Likely' due to COVID-19 Isolation Measures: ALERT," Global News, (June 26, 2020).

July, Cybertip.ca "reported an 81 per cent spike over April, May and June in reports from youth who had been sexually exploited, and reports of people trying to sexually abuse children."[193]

At the start of the lockdown, child advocates warned that child abuse cases would rise with the isolation measures it imposed.[194] The expectation was a common-sense one given that over 87 percent of cases of child abuse are perpetrated by people close to the children. Curiously, however, the cases of child abuse appear to have dropped in some jurisdictions, which may be related to the fact that the number of reports of child abuse is down. In Edmonton, reports of abuse declined by 31 percent from mid-March to mid-April.[195] It may well be that children are being better protected by their parents' close care during the confinement periods, but experts warn that the drop may be in fact bad news. "We still believe child abuse is going on, it's just not being reported" at the same rates, Sgt. Manuel Illner of the Edmonton Police Child Protection Section has said.[196] If this is true, as schools open up and some restrictions are lifted, we likely will see an increase in the number of reports of child abuse from previous months. Other jurisdictions have already noticed the intensity of abuse. For example, although the reported number of cases is lower at the Hospital for Children in Philadelphia, the teams that specialize in children's trauma, for instance, report an increase in the gravity of the cases they have seen in sexual and physical abuse during the beginning of the lockdown.[197]

---

[193] Elizabeth Thompson, "Child Sex Exploitation Is on the Rise in Canada during the Pandemic
Social Sharing," CBC News, (July 13, 2020).

[194] Michelle Ward, "Increase in Child Abuse a Big Concern during COVID-19 Pandemic," *Globe and Mail*, (March 20, 2020).

[195] Josée St-Onge, "Edmonton Sees Fewer Reports of Child Abuse during the COVID-19 Pandemic," CBC News, (April 29, 2020).

[196] Kendra Slugoski, "Child Abuse Reporting Down in Alberta amid COVID-19 and Agencies Warn That's Not a Good Thing," Global News, (April 28, 2020). A similar drop has been reported in New Brunswick. See Rachel Cave, "Reports of Suspected Child Abuse Have Fallen 40 Percent during COVID-19 Outbreak," CBC News, (April 15, 2020).

[197] Candy Woodall, "As Hospitals See More Severe Child Abuse Injuries during Coronavirus, 'The Worst is Yet to Come.'" *USA Today*, (May 13, 2020).

A similar report from the U.K. calls attention to a "surge in child abuse" for March and April.[198]

Regarding other indirect consequences from the pandemic, Deloitte released a paper entitled "Uncovering the Hidden Iceberg," calling attention to a looming crisis that would affect health levels and industrial productivity. If the effects of COVID-19 are similar to those of previous experiences of natural disasters and disruptions, an examination of the clinical psychology literature suggests that deep and prolonged effects will exist for some time to come.[199] To be sure, many of the drivers affecting mental health would be equally present in societies such as Sweden that did not engage in full lockdowns, but the stress brought on by the imposed confinement of suppressive strategies generates many more forms of stress, which makes matters worse.

On a different but closely related problem, Statistics Canada has released data showing increased numbers of deaths medically unrelated to the virus in British Columbia, Alberta, Quebec, and Ontario, the provinces most affected by COVID-19, that are not medically related to the virus. In addition, these "excess deaths" spiked in tandem with the propagation of the virus. The total number of computed "extra deaths" for these four provinces was initially reported to be 4,400 (with Ontario figures incomplete and Quebec's under-reported), which is roughly half the total of deaths registered in Canada at the height of the crisis.[200]

Statistics Canada reports that in British Columbia, the "excess mortality" detected over a six-week period starting in mid-March constituted "386 more deaths than in any of the previous five years for the same weeks." British Columbia COVID-19 deaths in the same time period this year were 99. In Quebec, from a 10-week period starting in mid-March, Statistics Canada found "3,384 more deaths in 2020 than in any of the previous five years," where 4,435 deaths were attributed to COVID-19. Statistics Canada expects the excess number of deaths to be revised upward because of delays in reporting in the latter portion of those 10

---

[198] Bridget M. Kuehn, "Surge in Child Abuse, Harm During COVID-19 Pandemic Reported," *JAMA Network*, (August 18, 2020).

[199] Deloitte, "Uncovering the Hidden Iceberg: Why the Human Impact of COVID-19 Could Be a Third Crisis," (August 2020).

[200] See Kenyon Wallace, "Canada's Four Largest Provinces Suffered More than 4400 Excess Deaths during Height of COVID-19 Pandemic, StatsCan Reports says," *Toronto Star*, (July 24, 2020).

weeks because of COVID-19 slowdowns. In Alberta, from the last week of February, there were "639 more deaths than the highest number recorded over the last 5 years" whereas 146 COVID-19 fatalities were recorded in that same period, 25 percent of "excess deaths." The Ontario data are incomplete, but the report's authors feel confident enough, given the national trend, that there is also a significant excess of deaths in Ontario.[201]

Statistics Canada did not speculate about the causes of these deaths. We expect that future analysis of the data will show that many of these deaths were related to delayed or avoided treatable illnesses, increased drug abuse (as we have already seen), suicides, etc., which are contingently related to the COVID-19 lockdown crisis.[202] Statistics Canada estimated that about a quarter of these excess deaths may be under-reported COVID-19 deaths. The same phenomenon has been observed elsewhere in the world. According to a BBC News report published on June 17, a review of data in several countries shows an excess of deaths at 130,000 contrasted to 440,000 COVID-19-related deaths reported at the time.[203] Excess deaths recorded in the United States were 26,986 as compared to 70,266 deaths from COVID-19;12,729 were counted as excess in the United Kingdom in relation to 51,804 assigned to COVID-19. For Sweden, between March 9 and May 17, 190 deaths are marked as excess in relation to the 3,981 COVID-19 reported deaths. Further analysis of the "excess deaths" data computed so far, in another BBC report, showed that England was the worst hit by this effect in Europe.[204] In countries where registration and reporting practices are less reliable, the discrepancies are much larger,

---

[201] Statistics Canada, "Provisional Death Counts and Excess Mortality, January 2019 to May 2020," (July 24, 2020).

[202] See also Gemma Postill et al., "An Analysis of Mortality in Ontario Using Cremation Data: Rise in Cremation during the COVID-19 Pandemic," *medRXiv* preprint, (July 24, 2020).

[203] Becky Dale and Nassos Stylianou, "Coronavirus: What is the True Death Toll of the Pandemic?" BBC News, (June 18, 2020). The BBC used a different method to calculate "excess deaths," but the results are equivalent, if not always comparable. They used the number of deaths expected based on previous years, contrasted with all the deaths thus far in 2020, from which they then subtracted the reported COVID-19 deaths. This assumed that all COVID-19 deaths are reported accurately, an assumption that is less certain in countries with poor record-keeping experience.

[204] Staff, BBC News, "Coronavirus: England Highest Level of Excess Deaths," (July 30, 2020).

suggesting that the number of COVID-19 reported deaths there is much less accurate. In Ecuador, for instance, the BBC reported 3,358 COVID-19 deaths and 16,107 excess deaths. Similarly, Chile had 1,053 COVID-19 deaths and 2,181 excess deaths.[205]

The main point of comparison, however, is that the proportional number of excess deaths in Sweden is lower in relation to COVID-19 deaths in Canada and many other lockdown states.[206] Moreover, Sweden has now experienced several weeks since June in which there were no excess deaths,[207] suggesting that COVID-19 deaths have been over-reported or that some of the elderly people who died from COVID-19 were among those who statistically would have died in the following weeks. As one Swedish doctor observed in mid-August: "Basically COVID is in all practical senses over and done in Sweden. After four months."[208]

Swedish authorities also reasoned that slowing down the advance of a virus through a tight lockdown experiment would not remove the threat or risk of the virus reappearing. In the absence of a vaccine, a resurgence would inevitably prompt another round of lockdowns, potentially trapping a society in a long and harmful cycle of lockdowns. The level of harm brought to people's health and the economy by recurring lockdowns would grow increasingly worse with each consecutive wave of restrictions, to say nothing of the potential increase in social and political unrest that later cycles might produce.

If no subsequent lockdowns would be tolerable, as in fact seems to be the case presently in many Western countries, one would be left in the same or in a very similar position as at the start of the crisis. As we noted above, the Swedish leadership concluded that this was not tolerable in a free society. Rashly imposing a lockdown only to end up more or less at the same place weeks and months later made no political sense and had no

---

[205] Becky Dale and Nassos Stylianou, "Coronavirus: What is the True Death Toll?"
[206] For a useful resource on "excess deaths" see Charlie Giattino, Hannah Ritchie, Max Roser et al., "Excess Mortality during the Coronavirus Pandemic (COVID-19)," *Our World in Data*, https://ourworldindata.org/excess-mortality-covid.
[207] Staff, Reuters, "Sweden Records First Week with No Excess Mortality since Pandemic Struck," (June 8, 2020); see also Emanuel Karlsten, "Number of Deaths in Sweden during the Pandemic – Compared to Previous Years' Mortality," (Sept. 1, 2020), emmanuelkarlsten.se.
[208] Sebastian Rushworth, "How Dangerous is COVID? A Swedish Doctor's Perspective," *Spectator*, (August 17, 2020).

reasonable justification. Given the unpredictable consequences and the availability of other options, such a course seems both futile and irresponsible. In other words, saving some lives at one end of the cycle while contributing to even more deaths and more unrelated suffering at the other end is not a strategy for success. The Swedes argued that when the locked-down countries opened up, "all those countries are going to end up with the same number of dead at the end of the day anyway."[209]

Tegnell echoed Rushworth's common sense. He mentioned in an interview with the *Washington Post* that Sweden's core mitigating strategy aimed at not having to shut down subsequent times.[210] The Swedish leadership considered the threat of COVID-19 over the long term strategically, thoughtfully, and in the light of rational premises. They did so without subscribing to a moral panic or by embracing ideological commitments. In a word, the Swedes were prudent because they fully considered the broad implications of the lockdown alternative, an approach conspicuously absent among those who chose the lockdown option. In addition, the Swedish strategy retained a local input and did not overrule the common sense and prudence of local authorities. Less than a month into the lockdown, Lars Løkke Rasmussen, a Danish member of parliament and the former Liberal prime minister of Denmark, voiced his concern for the small merchants and businesspeople. He also expressed his skepticism with the lockdowns and what he perceived as the mission creep in his country's suppression strategy; namely, "that people do not get sick." He reflected that if that was the goal, "we must not open society at all." Rasmussen was aware of the faulty logic that led to bureaucratic mission creep as the lockdown strategy developed in a direction that aimed at the impossible goal of people not getting sick. Moreover, he was aware of the consequences: "It is [a matter of] life or death. And so it is — on a smaller scale — also for the entrepreneur, the hairdresser, the masseur, the restaurateur. All those who keep the wheels turning and earn the money that we now generously spend on relief packages." Rasmussen also allowed that even if the panic-driven lockdown may have been understandable, considering that a decision needed to be made quickly to protect lives, he

[209] Sebastian Rushworth, "How Dangerous is COVID?"
[210] Michael Birnbaum, "Scientist behind Sweden's Covid-19 Strategy Suggests It Allowed Too Many Deaths."

still wondered why his country continued to pursue an unsustainable option, particularly after the costs became so evident.[211]

The reasoned common-sense basis on which Sweden began to deal with the crisis, absent the moral panic we have seen elsewhere, was widely deemed callous and irresponsible. Thus, Matt Gurney wrote in the *National Post* (June 4, 2020) that Sweden's strategy "didn't work." Most of the world locked down hard to preserve health-care systems and buy time to study the virus and its effect on humans. Sweden chose "a far more liberal course and paid for it in lives relative to their peers [in Scandinavia], but did not escape the economic consequences or achieve herd immunity. By any metric, this is a failure. Sweden stoically took the pain but realized no gain." The decision to let the virus move through the population when combined with mitigating measures to protect those most at risk aimed at building up collective or "herd" immunity. The Swedish plan never involved stopping the virus. But it never meant doing nothing, either.

It may be too early to draw definitive conclusions regarding the success or failure for either the suppressive or the mitigating strategies; however, one can say with confidence that the preliminary results are mixed. The evaluation of any strategy should not be based on its intentions, but on its implementation and its outcomes; that is, on whether it accomplished its stated initial objectives, and whether it did so with minimum collateral damage. Both strategies have similar life-saving goals but involve radically different approaches and expectations. The suppressive strategy was initially presented as a reasonable way "to flatten the curve." It originally aimed at slowing the virus's spread so that the infections would not overwhelm the medical system, which in turn would save lives. The central focus was the protection of the medical system, and in that context, "flattening the curve" made sense. The desired metrics for evaluating success was the capacity to maintain the integrity of medical services and manage the number of deaths. It never aimed at stopping all deaths from the virus but almost all lockdown strategies never included an exit plan, let alone an exit strategy. The mitigating strategy that Sweden employed also sought to slow transmission in order to protect the medical system's ability to look after the sick and protect the vulnerable as much as possible, but it would also allow the virus to move through the population so that

---

[211] Lars Løkke Rasmussen, "I'm Not Sure We're Pursuing the Right Strategy," *Berlingske*, (April 7, 2020).

collective immunities would develop. In this way, life in Sweden could continue with a large degree of normalcy. The Swedes meant to cover a much wider range of health issues than only fighting SARS-CoV-2, and carefully considered consequences of their actions as well as the question of how to end the restrictions.

As we write in the fall of 2020, Sweden had slowed the infection rates, and managed, and controlled the number of critical cases and deaths.[212] Although Sweden has been harshly criticized for having a higher rate of deaths in relation to population than some European countries, by the end of summer 2020 it had reduced the number of deaths, almost at the same time as several European countries and domestic jurisdictions that opted for the lockdown. What is more, by the end of September 2020, Sweden was experiencing a lower rate of infection, a lower number of hospitalizations, and a lower number of daily deaths than many European countries that had initially achieved lower mortality rates than Sweden. Most significantly, also at the end of September 2020, several countries that had locked down and then reopened were anticipating a second wave of infection and were initiating tighter restrictions and a second round of lockdowns. In four of these countries, full or partial lockdowns had been reinstated weeks after being lifted: Australia, New Zealand, Israel, and Canada (Quebec and Ontario).[213] This was why Rushworth noted that even though "Sweden has one of the highest total death rates in the world," nevertheless, "COVID is over in Sweden."[214]

For those following a suppression strategy, once the first objective was secured and the curve was flattened, the goal changed to ensuring that no one would contract the virus, undoubtedly under the fear of a post-lockdown surge causing a second wave. Nowhere was this more evident

---

[212] *Medscape*, (August 19, 2020); (September 8, 2020).

[213] Ahead of the official announcements from Quebec and Ontario, which have constitutional jurisdiction over health, the prime minister jumped the gun and declared that Alberta, Ontario, and Quebec were already in a second wave of infection. That seems to have been the case for the two Laurentian provinces. Deena Hinshaw, chief medical officer of health in Alberta, publicly contradicted the prime minister within a day, and offered a more sober assessment of the situation in her province. She mentioned that Alberta has not experienced second-wave conditions and may not see a spike in infections substantive enough to constitute a second wave. See CBC News, "Alberta Not in 2nd Wave of Pandemic, Top Doctor Says," (September 25, 2020).

[214] Sebastian Rushworth, "How Dangerous is COVID?"

than in New Zealand, where the country's prime minister ordered the city of Auckland re-locked down in August upon the appearance of 30 new cases. New Zealand had originally locked down on March 25, 2020. The prime minister's stated but impossible objective was to be rid of the virus. "Together, we have got rid of COVID before," Jacinda Ardern said, evidently unaware of the irony of her statement. "We have kept it out for 102 days, longer than any other country. We have been world-leading in our COVID response, with the result that many lives were saved and our economy was getting going faster than almost anywhere else. We can do all of that again."[215] In early June, Ardern "did a little dance" and declared the country "COVID-19 free." At the time, New Zealand had had "1,154 confirmed cases and 22 deaths" in the whole country with a population of five million.[216] She did not say how many times the New Zealand government was prepared to lock down its citizens again with each detection of new cases. But given that the appearance of 30 new infections was deemed serious enough to relaunch a lockdown in a major modern city of a developed country, almost any number thereafter would trigger the same reaction. Therein lies the unsustainable aspect of the lockdown policy when it turned into an effort to extinguish the virus. Witness a budding manifestation of the same disposition in the alarmist CBC headline about Canada's smallest province, Prince Edward Island: "1 New Case of COVID-19 Confirmed on P.E.I."[217] The logic of suppression seems to lead many to the impossible wish for eradication. If it were only a wish, there would be no harm done. The problem, however, is that decision-makers conclude that the virus can be eradicated by hiding from it. Consider that the last recorded incidence of an infection by the H1N1 strain — which between 1918 and 1920 caused the so-called Spanish flu — was in the 1950s.

---

[215] Nick Perry, "New Zealand Extends Auckland Lockdown as Virus Cluster Grows," CTV News, (August 14, 2020).

[216] Staff, BBC News, "New Zealand Lifts All COVID Restrictions, Declaring the Nation Virus-free," (June 8, 2020).

[217] Sheehan Desjardins, "1 New Case of COVID-19 Confirmed on P.E.I.," CBC News (PEI), (September 23, 2020). It would be too simple to dismiss this reaction as the type coming from a small town. This was Canada's national broadcaster. How precarious do things need to be in the mind of a CBC editor that one new case in a province leads to the special attention of a news report with such an alarming tone? We discuss other examples of media sensationalism below.

On September 18, the government of Israel announced a second and new lockdown for the following three weeks, just at the beginning of Rosh Hashanah. The new lockdown came four months after the end of the first one. While the new lockdown was not as stringent as the one initiated in March — for which the Israeli authorities boasted that they had worked in close partnership with the Chinese government — there are some signs of unrest and opposition was mounting among religious groups, the tourism and hospitality industry, and restaurant and shop owners. This should be of some concern to Laurentian Canadians looking to lock down again.

On the first weekend of the second lockdown in Israel, there was much defiance. Restaurants opened in protest, despite fines of US$1,500 per day, and religious gatherings and mass protests organized in defiance of the new orders. Over 7,000 police officers patrolled the streets and manned checkpoints. They handed down close to 5,000 fines to people violating the one-kilometre radius from their domicile that the new rules permitted and close to 200 fines for individuals failing to wear masks in public. Some restaurant owners were arrested for refusing to close their business.[218] Given increased enforcement and increased levels of resistance, civil disobedience and discontent may grow to levels more difficult to manage.

In Canada, between late July and September 2020, media reports focused on the growing number of COVID-19 cases, but did not seem to pay nearly as much attention to the state of the health system or the fact that as the number of infections increased, the number of critical patients and deaths fell and in some jurisdictions nearly disappeared. Indeed, reacting to the increased numbers of COVID-19 infections in their province, Quebec politicians mused about granting greater police powers, including the power to violate private domiciles to stop gatherings that break a new 10-person limit (*National Post*, September 16, 2020). It seems obvious to us that the rhetoric of panic is misguided, given that infections do not equal hospitalizations, and hospitalizations do not equal deaths. Ironically, the new measures were being discussed only weeks before the 50th anniversary of the October Crisis, a vivid chapter in Quebec history. Half a century ago, the province and the country were sent into a real crisis when a terrorist cell for the Front de Libération du Québec (FLQ) kidnapped Pierre Laporte, Quebec's minister of labour, and James Cross,

---

[218] Staff, *Times of Israel*, "Business Owners Rebel against New Lockdown Restrictions," (September 21, 2020); and Ibid., "Police Checkpoints Jam Roads as Israelis Go Back to Work under Lockdown," (September 21, 2020).

the British trade commissioner. Laporte was later murdered. Reacting to the kidnappings, then-prime minister Pierre Trudeau sent troops into the streets of Montreal as if it were Northern Ireland. Surviving Quebecers still recall countless violations of fundamental rights against so many poets, journalists, academics, and artists suspected of sympathizing with the separatist terrorists.

Next door, Premier Doug Ford's alarming rhetoric has been trying to scare Ontarians into compliance. On September 14, Ford added to the COVID-19 panic in his province. Following 31,143 tests and 313 new cases (one percent of those tested), Ford invoked a dreaded second COVID-19 wave: "I believe it is coming as sure as I am standing here." He also raised the threat of a new lockdown: "… every option is on the table. We will take up every step necessary, including further shutdowns." By September, after being politically embarrassed in May 2020 when testing in his province fell short of what he had promised, Ford boasted that Ontario leads Canada, reaching 40,000 and aiming at 50,000 daily tests. The connection between "hammering the testing," as Ford described his policy, and the infection increases seems to be ignored. As previously stated, the more tests, the more cases of infection are discovered.

Alarmist headlines emphasizing case growth will scare some but will only harden existing skeptics and create new ones. People can read and are able to tell the difference between the rate of infection leading to higher numbers of cases and the actual number of people admitted to hospital because they contracted the virus. On September 22, 478 new cases were reported, but there were only 82 COVID-19 patients in all Ontario hospitals. There is a legitimate concern in that this number doubled since September 13, and that is fair. But of the 82 who were hospitalized by September 22, 24 were in intensive care, with 11 of them on ventilators. In addition, of the 478 new cases, eight people were aged over 80, the most critically vulnerable, and three new COVID-19 deaths were reported in a population of nearly 15 million people. One does not have to be unsympathetic to the 24 people in intensive care to mention that the overblown emphasis on infection numbers is practically meaningless except for unnecessarily increasing fear.

This does not mean that increasing fear among the general population does not in some sense work. From the beginning, the Trudeau government's evident strategy has been to present a "stark choice — either selflessly shut down the economy to save lives or selfishly worry about the economy and condemn thousands to a vicious illness" (*National Post*, May 16, 2020). Randall Denley, writing in the *National Post* (May 22, 2020) clearly spelled out the effect of inducing a moral panic: "Ontario's economy can't restart effectively without schools and daycares being open — and fully attended. That's not going to happen until parents are confident that their children can return to school with minimal risk." A measure of the success of inducing fear among citizens is that by early August, "more than half of Canadians fear returning to the office" (*National Post*, August 7, 2020) and large numbers of Ontario parents were afraid to send their kids back to school (*National Post*, August 28, 2020). Despite the deliberate induction of fear by various governments in Canada, it is not clear that providing exaggerated information or presenting accurate information in ways that exaggerate the danger may only work in the short term. It certainly worked in March in the early days of the lockdown and may still be working in August, but it cannot work forever and usually backfires when people learn to mistrust and ignore both message and messenger. This is the common-sense wisdom exemplified in Aesop's fable, "The Boy Who Cried Wolf."

Ontarians in particular should be concerned with the escalating language and condescending vitriol toward challengers, skeptics, and rule-breakers. On September 21, responding to questions about "clamping down," Ford implied that people who attended an event in Ancaster were "brainless," and vowed to track them down for "putting people's lives in jeopardy." There is no evidence that the alleged brainless citizens have infected anyone, yet Ford's comments pave the way for unleashing coercive machinery against those who may legitimately disagree with his inflated, panic-inducing, medical rhetoric. His evident instinct was to punish others and paint himself as a saviour.

Ford is not alone. Moreover, precisely because he is not alone, his message and tone will resonate among many, especially when the media amplify it. As if modellers were not discredited enough after Ferguson's disastrous predictions, CBC's Laura Glowacki found Robert Smith? (the question mark is part of his name). Smith? is a mathematician at the University of Ottawa and builds models for infectious diseases. He called for a "ruthless" and "draconian" return to a full lockdown "for a few months … [that] … could bring numbers down to zero new infections."[219] In reality, the objective of achieving zero infections is impossible. In Alberta, similarly, there are attempts at creating something like zero-infection zones. If one or two people at a school, whether staff or pupils, were detected with COVID-19 following the relaxed lockdown rules for opening schools in September 2020, this would now be considered "an outbreak," which may be considered sufficient reason to close down a whole school. Unless there is a rational perspective about what the rising number of infection cases really means, and unless there are reasonable mitigating strategies to protect the vulnerable, the alarmist rhetoric will likely panic the largest province in the country into another harmful lockdown while simultaneously causing an increase in skepticism, challenges, and resistance. As Tegnell understood: "Temporary lockdowns will ultimately backfire."

Indeed, the number of deaths per million inhabitants and the number of critical cases at the end of the summer of 2020 show the differences between the mitigating and the suppressive approaches. As of September 24, 2020, Sweden had counted 90,923 cases of COVID-19, which had produced 5,880 casualties. Deaths per million inhabitants in Sweden were at 581, making it the 11th largest death rate in the world at the time of writing.[220] Belgium led that category among European countries with 858 deaths per million (one less than reported in late August), followed by Spain with 665, the United Kingdom with 616, and Italy in fourth place with 592. France had 482. Sweden's neighbours, Norway, Denmark, and Finland had then among the lowest deaths per million with 50, 111, and 62, respectively. For further reference, Canada and the United States had 244 and 635 deaths per million, respectively. In terms of numbers of critical patients by September 24, it was as follows: Spain with 1,445, France with 951, Italy with 246, U.K. with 211, Belgium with 95, and Sweden with 15. Norway, Denmark, and Finland had two, 14, and four, respectively. Canada and the United States had 86 and 14,090 critically hospitalized cases, respectively.

---

[219] Cited in Laura Glowacki, "Experts Call for Lockdown Measures Now to Deal with COVID-19 Surge," CBC News, (September 25, 2020).

[220] When we first looked at these figures in late August 2020, Sweden was fifth in the world in terms of deaths per million. One month later, it had dropped six places. Among European countries, it was in fifth place on September 24, 2020.

Notwithstanding that Sweden is not far from the European average of deaths per million,[221] critics of the Swedish mitigation strategy point at the contrast in the number of deaths per million between Sweden and Norway, for instance, to signal the failure of the Swedish approach. In some ways, they would rather interpret the results in Italy, Spain, the U.K., and Belgium as exceptions to the lockdown (and perhaps they are). They would rather ignore the fact that these four European states, which are among those who imposed the strictest lockdown conditions in Europe with curfews and police arrests, have surpassed Sweden in deaths per million. The lockdowns in Spain and Italy were particularly tight. In Belgium, there are reports of people being monitored by aerial drones,[222] with hundreds of fines handed out and citizens placed in "administrative detentions" a mere week into the lockdown.[223] None of these things occurred in Sweden, though some businesses have been fined for violating directives related to distancing inside restaurants.

It is not our intention to compare Sweden to Canada directly. Given land mass, population size, distribution, density, and so on, meaningful comparison is difficult. Nor is it useful to compare Sweden's COVID-19 death rate to Alberta's, which the Alberta government did in an attempt to justify its lockdown actions. Saving lives is a powerful justification to violate norms of civil liberties and constitutional rights.[224] Nevertheless, if one wished to compare a Canadian province to Sweden, one might as well use one with comparable numbers of inhabitants, an older demographic, and a more urban concentration. A comparison between Sweden and Quebec, for instance, may be quite appropriate in relation to what the critics identify as an elevated death rate in Sweden among senior residents in long-term care facilities and retirement homes. Considering that the

---

[221] Johan Norberg, "In Sweden, Will Voluntary Self-Isolation Work Better than State-Enforced Lockdowns in the Long Run?" *Reason*, (April 17, 2020).
[222] Gavin Lee, "Coronavirus: Why So Many People are Dying in Belgium," BBC News (Brussels), (May 2, 2020).
[223] Gabriela Galindo, "Hundreds of Reports Issued as Police Chase Lockdown Violators," *Brussels Times*, (March 23, 2020).
[224] To see Alberta compared to Sweden, go to the government of Alberta's website at https://www.alberta.ca/assets/documents/covid19-cases-alberta-vs-sweden.pdf. The three-page PDF has the litigious sounding title "Alberta vs. Sweden." n.d.; Allison Bench, "Why a Less Restrictive COVID-19 Approach like Sweden's Wasn't Used in Alberta," Global News, (May 25, 2020).

stated objective of both experiments has been the protection of the most vulnerable among their populations, and the elderly were identified from the start as being in the vulnerable category, such a comparison is legitimate. The SARS-CoV-2 virus is particularly lethal to people with health vulnerabilities and co-morbidities, including respiratory problems, obesity, immunodeficiencies, and so on.

In Sweden, 96 percent of the COVID-19 deaths (by mid-August 2020) have occurred among those aged 60 and above. This has been rightly identified as the single greatest failure of the Swedish strategy, as Tegnell acknowledged. Overall, in Canada, 97.09 percent of COVID-19 deaths as of August 4, 2020 were people aged 60 and older. Quebec, with a strict suppressive lockdown had 97.8 per cent of its COVID-19 deaths among the demographic of 60 and above.[225] Similarly, other jurisdictions in North America have failed miserably to protect their elderly (New York State immediately comes to mind). Therefore, it is premature to say on the one hand that the Swedish experiment has been callous and irresponsible because of the number of deaths among its elderly population and even more so to suggest that the high death toll among the elderly is inherent to the mitigating strategy. Even months after strong intervention by the Canadian Armed Forces, Ontario and Quebec continue to struggle with protecting elderly residents in long-term care centres.[226] *Maclean's* reported

---

[225] At one point, Quebec stationed police on the border with Ontario to prevent Ontarians from entering the province. Such border restrictions were unconstitutional in two ways: they violated s.6 (2)(a) of the *Charter*, which guarantees freedom of movement between provinces, and they usurped the federal government's jurisdiction to regulate interprovincial travel. New Brunswick was also criticized because that province delegated its illegal closure to a private non-governmental organization, the Red Cross, and instructed it to enforce the blockade without the possibility of appeal (*National Post*, June 10, 2020).

[226] The Canadian Armed Forces found deplorable conditions among several long-term centres in the Laurentian provinces, which they carefully documented. There needs to be a serious reckoning in Canada about the way the elderly in need of medical care are warehoused at some of these facilities. Copies of the Canadian Armed Forces' reports regarding the dire conditions that soldiers found inside long-term care facilities in Quebec and in Ontario have been posted online. The report for Ontario can be found here http://s3.documentcloud.org/documents/6928480/OP-LASER-JTFC-Observations-in-LTCF-in-On.pdf and the report for Quebec (en français) is here: https://cdn-contenu.quebec.ca/cdn-contenu/sante/documents/Problemes_de_sante/covid-

that as of September 8, "Ontario has 19 active outbreaks at LTC facilities. The two worst were in the Ottawa area; they have recorded the deaths of 71 residents to date. Quebec also has 19 active LTC outbreaks in its province; its two worst LTC outbreaks are in Montreal; they account for 182 deaths."[227] By the end of September, there were 46 active outbreaks in long-term care centres in Ontario.[228] From this perspective, Canadians are in no position to criticize the Swedish experiment. We are not cherry-picking jurisdictions with lockdowns that have performed poorly. The point is that the expectation of massive failure for Sweden's soft touch did not materialize. With all its acknowledged mistakes, Sweden still outperformed several European states. That is the surprising news we seldom hear. Moreover, as second waves threaten to induce a few countries to impose second lockdowns, Sweden's comparative standing among its neighbours is bound to improve.

John Miltimore of the Foundation for Economic Education argued that a fairer measure of the Swedish approach is to look at the early model predictions. Expectations based on the Ferguson Imperial College model predicted the collapse of intensive care units (ICUs) in Sweden before the beginning of May and said that close to 100,000 people would perish from COVID-19 by July.[229] Sweden's 5,878 deaths (by September 24) pale in comparison to the anticipated carnage that the Ferguson model expected. Similarly, Sweden's health-care system was never overwhelmed, let alone in danger of collapsing. Contrary to all expectation, it seems, the rate of infection has slowed and is smaller (as we write) than in Britain, France, Spain, and other European nations which seem to be experiencing a surge, perhaps even a second wave. Likewise, for parts of Laurentian Canada: both Quebec and Ontario went into (partial) lockdowns again at the end

---

19/Rapport_FAC/Observation_FAC_CHSLD.pdf?1590587216. Ontario Premier Doug Ford has ordered an investigation into the high incidence of deaths in retirement homes and long-term care facilities, and into the conditions leading to these deaths in his province.

[227] Patricia Treble, "Coronavirus in Canada: These Charts Show How Our Fight to 'Flatten the Curve' is Going," *Maclean's*, (September 10, 2020).

[228] Government of Ontario, "Data Catalogue: Long-Term Care Home COVID-19 Data," https://data.ontario.ca/dataset/long-term-care-home-covid-19-data; see also Chris Fox, "Visitors Will be Restricted at Long-term Care Homes in Some Regions Starting Next Week," CP24, (September 29, 2020).

[229] Jon Miltimore, "Sweden's Actual COVID-19 Results Compared to What Modellers Predicted in April," Foundation for Economic Education, (July 29, 2020).

of September 2020. In response, 20 doctors and professors of medicine signed a (once again poorly written) open letter to Ford arguing against a general re-lockdown. "It's time to do something different," they concluded.[230] At the same time, the number of deaths in Sweden has dropped significantly, as has the number of critical cases requiring acute care. The daily cumulative average of deaths for a seven-day period leading up to September 23 was one, whereas the U.K. had 37, Russia had 150, Italy had 20, France had 43, Spain had 130, and Israel (then under second lockdown) had 40. Canada had nine. Regardless of population size, recall again that Sweden did not lock down and the others did.[231]

This does not mean Sweden is out of the woods or that they expect the virus will be eradicated in that country. But with a likely rate of infection approaching one in five people in the Stockholm area, where the vast majority of the Swedish cases have occurred, Sweden may be closer to a return to normality, and better prepared to reopen fully. That is, the Swedes have good reason to experience fewer worries and anticipate less long-term impact on their population than many of the lockdown states now filled with anxieties over the prospect of an even worse second wave of infections and a greater number of deaths.

For those whose models predicted the destruction of Sweden when the country chose not to pursue a suppressive lockdown, the contagion rate inexplicably peaked in mid-June and slowed down thereafter. The number of people being admitted to hospital and the number of people needing intensive care declined, which in turn influenced the pronounced drop in the number of deaths that had peaked in mid-April. The slow but continuous drop in the number of seriously sick people and the reduction in the number of deaths could not be explained with any scientific rigour inside the lockdown framework. Swedish authorities began quietly to float the idea that by mid-July, Sweden was close to reaching herd immunity.[232] As Rushworth observed, "if herd immunity hasn't developed, where are all the sick people?"[233] Some observers believed that the decline in hospitalizations and deaths in Sweden was caused by simple environmental factors such as summer heat and greater outdoor living during the summer

---

[230] *National Post*, (October 1, 2020).
[231] See Worldometers, https://www.worldometers.info/coronavirus/.
[232] Staff, Reuters, "Swedish Epidemiology Boss Says Questioned COVID-19 Strategy Seems to be Working," (July 21, 2020).
[233] Sebastian Rushworth, "How Dangerous is COVID?"

months. At issue therefore is the status of Swedish herd immunity that we discussed above.

The concept is not without controversy. There is some contention as to what level of infection constitutes a "large part" in a community for it to reach herd immunity. This is normally called the "herd immunity threshold." At the end of April, the WHO released a scientific brief, calling into question the feasibility of herd immunity. The brief discussed immunity from COVID-19 in relation to issuing "immunity passports."[234] An immunity passport assumed the continuation of a lockdown, but granted authorities the power to issue certificates for survivors who demonstrably had acquired post-infection COVID-19 immunity. They could then return to work while the lockdown continued for everyone else and circulate with few restrictions. After a short discussion of how immunities could be achieved, the WHO brief cast doubt on whether immunity from COVID-19 was even possible in the mid- to long term: "As of April 24th, 2020, no study has evaluated whether the presence of antibodies to SARS-CoV-2 confers immunity to subsequent infection by this virus in humans." The observation may have been true, but the articulation of skepticism within the WHO also cast doubt on the Swedish mitigating strategy that was generally interpreted to pursue herd immunity as its central goal. In addition, the WHO's skepticism tacitly endorsed the lockdown approach.

In other words, the WHO was suggesting that people infected with SARS-CoV-2 could catch it again within an unspecified amount of time. The brief further fueled anxiety by leaving open the probability that without a vaccine, people could be trapped in an endless pandemic infection lockdown loop. It suggested a kind of COVID-19 "Groundhog Day," reminiscent of the 1993 movie in which a narcissistic TV weatherman played by Bill Murray is trapped in Punxsutawney, Pennsylvania, day after day reliving Groundhog Day in a recurrent cycle until he learns the lessons of decency that he needs to learn. The movie was a comedy, but the equivalent image of being trapped in cycles of viral infection in the absence of immunity until science liberates us from such purgatory was terrifying to many.

---

[234] World Health Organization, "'Immunity Passports' in the Context of COVID-19," (April 24, 2020). It should come as no surprise that lockdown advocates such as Alberta's chief medical officer of health, Deena Hinshaw, were opposed to the very notion of herd immunity. Global News, (September 28, 2020).

Other experts correctly noted that, like any organism, the coronavirus mutates. This basic biological fact was then given an alarmist interpretation: as humans become immune, through either infections or vaccines, "the virus could be under selective pressure to evade the human immune response." It could. Or maybe not, since it is hardly clear what the effective response of the mutations is. Even so, the emphasis is on the worst possible outcome. David Movens, an immunologist at the U.S. National Institute of Allergy and Infectious Diseases said: "although we don't know yet, it is well within the realm of possibility that this coronavirus, when our population-level immunity gets high enough, this coronavirus will find a way to get around our immunity" (*National Post*, September 24, 2020). Secretary General of the United Nations António Guterres added his voice to the alarm: "The outbreak remains out of control. The world is burning" (*Financial Post*, September 18, 2020). He then linked "recovery" to ending climate change and the use of fossil fuels: "Recovery must be green ... Recovery must advance gender equality. And recovery requires effective multilateralism." Mission creep is clearly endemic to international bureaucrats at the UN, but Guterres' aspirations seem over the top even for a secretary general.

The debate about immunity has persisted and it raises interesting issues and additional uncertainties. It has become focused on the question of antibodies. When a person has been infected, the immune system generates antibodies against the pathogen and antibodies remain in one's system for some time, rendering the person immune. Measuring the presence of antibodies would reveal the depth of the contagion. Accordingly, several countries began testing for antibodies to gauge the advance of the infection. This was important because a good portion of the population was said to have been infected without manifesting any symptoms. These were the notorious asymptomatic cases that the media declared during the early days of the pandemic to be a novel attribute of COVID-19 as though no other coronavirus had ever before infected people without generating symptoms. Testing for the virus and for antibodies in Sweden revealed that the number of people infected had reached 10-15 percent by May, a number that was nowhere near the much higher expected herd immunity requirements. In consequence, many observers claimed that Sweden must have failed to reach herd immunity by then. In fact, because there was no consensus on the immunity threshold, there could be no consensus on the timeline for community immunity so that no one knew when or at what rate it would be reached. That did not stop lockdown enthusiasts from declaring the impossibility of reaching it, or from announcing at several points that Sweden had failed.[235]

The second important question was whether immunity, if achieved, lasted long enough to establish stable community immunity. As to the threshold issue, some have suggested it is only reached at numbers as high as 90 percent infection among the population.[236] Others say that it takes 50 to 60 percent. Haley E. Randolph and Luis B. Barreiro from Genetics, Genomics, and Systems Biology at the University of Chicago published last May in *Immunity* a paper entitled "Herd Immunity: Understanding COVID-19." It presented a statistical model showing that a 67 percent infection rate constituted a plausible immunity threshold for the SARS-CoV-2 virus.[237] The paper also argued that "there is no straightforward, ethical path to reach this goal [herd immunity], as the societal consequences of achieving it are devastating." We will return to this last point. In mid-August, similarly, *Science* published a paper modelling an immunity threshold for SARS-CoV-2 at approximately 40 percent based

---

[235] Eric J. W. Orlowski and David J. A. Goldsmith, "Four Months into the COVID-19 Pandemic, Sweden's Prized Herd Immunity is Nowhere in Sight," *Journal of the Royal Society of Medicine*, (August 11, 2020); Laurie Garrett and John Moore, "Herd Immunity Works—If You Don't Care How Many People Die," *Fortune*, (July 27, 2020); Marina Pollán, Beatriz Pérez-Gómez, et al., "Prevalence of SARS-CoV-2 in Spain (ENE-COVID): A Nationwide, Population-based Seroepidemiological Study," *Lancet*, 396:10250, (July 6, 2020); Rupert Steiner, "Sweden is Developing Herd Immunity, Some of the Country's Experts Claim, But the Figures Say Otherwise," *Market Watch*, (September 4, 2020); Jacqueline Howard, "A Herd Immunity Strategy to Fight the Pandemic Can be 'Dangerous,' Experts Say. Here's Why," CNN, (September 1, 2020); Sinéad Baker, "The Architect of Sweden's No-lockdown Strategy Said Up to 30% of its Population Could Now Be Immune to COVID-19, a Claim Backed Up by Little Data," *Business Insider*, (August 10, 2020); James Savage, "How Sweden's Herd Immunity Strategy has Backfired," *New Statesman*, (June 11, 2020). Mike Ryan, director of the WHO's Health Emergencies Program, said "no one is safe until everyone is safe" and that it was dangerous to think that countries could "magically reach herd immunity." *National Post*, (May 13, 2020).
[236] See Gypsyamber D'Souza and David Dowdy, "What is Herd Immunity and How Can We Achieve it With COVID-19?" Johns Hopkins Bloomberg School of Public Health, (April 10, 2020).
[237] Haley E. Randolph and Luis B. Barreiro, "Herd Immunity: Understanding COVID-19," *Immunity*, (May 19, 2020).

on different population heterogeneity assumptions that accounted for age and activity.[238] Their reasoning is worth considering. They began with a conventional definition of herd immunity: "a level of population immunity at which disease spreading will decline and stop even after all preventive measures have been relaxed."[239] Obviously, "if all preventive measures have been relaxed when the immunity level from infection is below the herd immunity level," then the anticipated second wave of infection may start once restrictions such as a lockdown are lifted. For COVID-19, the "classical" herd immunity level was estimated at between 50 percent and 75 percent and could not be achieved (as Ferguson and many others argued) without unacceptably high case fatality levels.

However: "no realistic model will depict human populations as homogeneous," which means that the "classical" models are not realistic. When these simple models are made more realistic — and the authors introduce only two additional variables (heterogeneous age distributions and social activity levels), the result of such a slightly greater approximation to reality is that the "disease-induced herd immunity level may be substantially lower than the classic herd immunity level derived from mathematical models assuming homogeneous immunization."[240] That is, the introduction of two additional factors (and in reality there are far more than two) was simply illustrative: the reduction went from around 60 percent to 43 percent. If other attributes could be modelled reliably (such as distribution of robustness of individual immune systems), the number could conceivably drop even more.

While there is no consensus yet about what constitutes a SARS-CoV-2 immunity threshold, it was accepted that a majority of the community needed to be infected. It largely rested on the claim regarding the "novelty" of the virus, which early on received the name "new coronavirus." It makes the somewhat reasonable assumption that because our medical officials have declared it to be new, it must also be new to our immune systems. The alleged novelty meant that the community immunity for it would have to be built, as it were, from zero to whatever number one could reasonably pick above 50 percent. In addition, the speed at which community

---

[238] See Tom Britton, Frank Ball, and Pieter Trapman, "A Mathematical Model Reveals the Influence of Population Heterogeneity on Herd Immunity to SARS-CoV-2," *Science*, vol. 369, 6505, (August 14, 2020): 846–849.

[239] Ibid., 846.

[240] Ibid., 848.

immunity could be achieved was another element to argue about because it rested on the rate of infection in a population. The Swedish strategy sought to slow down the infection rate to ensure the reliability and quality of medical care for the very sick from SARS-CoV-2, but otherwise would let the virus move through the community to develop immunity, assuming that the immunity holds.

Accordingly, a cluster of recent studies focused on the question of immunities based on antibodies to SARS-CoV-2. One hopeful study by a team of scientists largely from the Beijing Key Laboratory for Animal Models of Emerging and Remerging Infectious Diseases revealed in mid-March that some immunity to SARS-CoV-2 could be reached. Their experiment with simians showed that SARS-CoV-2 could not be retransmitted a month after infection.[241] In June 2020, a subsequent study demonstrated that antibodies produced by people infected with SARS-CoV-2 lingered in the body post-infection from between 47 to 75 days. The study also determined that the SARS-CoV-2 antibodies offered "no cross-reactivity … with several known circulating coronaviruses."[242] Essentially, that meant that antibody immunities developed from other more common coronaviruses were useless in the fight against COVID-19. Other studies questioned this conclusion.

More recent studies, for example, have demonstrated greater immunity durability. Tyler J. Ripperger and colleagues have published a study that demonstrates that immunity to SARS-CoV-2 can endure for several months in those who have been infected.[243] Only days later, a Canadian research team found in another not yet peer-reviewed study that antibodies for COVID-19 persisted in the bodies of infected persons, however mild or acute the infection, for about three months.[244] Establishing the probability of short-term immunity may lead to a short-term community

---

[241] Linlin Bao, Wei Deng, et al., "Lack of Reinfection in Rhesus Macaques Infected with SARS-CoV-2," *bioRXiv*, (May 1, 2020).

[242] Anita S. Iyer et al., "Dynamics and Significance of the Antibody Response to SARS-CoV-2 Infection," *medRXiv*, (July 20, 2020).

[243] Tyler J. Ripperger et al., "Detection, Prevalence, and Duration of Humoral Responses to SARS-CoV-2 under Conditions of Limited Population Exposure," *medRXiv*, (August 16, 2020).

[244] Baweleta Isho, Kento T. Abe, et al., "Mucosal Versus Systemic Antibody Responses to SARS-CoV-2 Antigens in COVID-19 Patients," *medRXiv*, (August 29, 2020).

immunity strategy, but it left unanswered the question as to the staying power of the antibodies that produced the immunity. Previous serology research done on SARS patients had shown that immunity could persist for about two years, but the concerns about the duration of the immunity remained. Studies from early summer of 2020 have found that immunity to SARS-CoV-2 weakens or disappears inside of a year and generally established "that asymptomatic individuals had a weaker immune response to SARS-CoV-2 infection."[245] The typical immunity duration from a common cold, which as mentioned earlier is induced by four different types of coronaviruses, is about six months according to a study published in May 2020 as the culmination of 35 years of research.[246] This study implied that without vaccine-induced immunity, the world would be subject to returning cycles of SARS-CoV-2 infection akin to the cycles of common influenza. The implications regarding the success of lockdowns were dire.

Antibody tests on population samples in the U.S. show much lower levels of infection than would be required for herd immunity, but antibody counts may not tell the whole story in several senses. First, antibody tests may lead to underestimation of cases because (1) they are not sensitive enough to detect mild COVID-19 cases that produce low levels of antibodies, (2) most antibody tests overlook the first line of defence against viruses and bacteria called IgA, and (3) many people show immunological response to SARS-CoV-2 in their T cells without having antibodies in their blood.[247]

The last observation regarding T cells was particularly significant. At the end of June 2020, an international group affiliated with Stockholm's Karolinska Institute published results of a study focused on the function of T cells, rather than on antibodies, in the immune systems of persons

---

[245] Long, Q., X. Tang, Q. Shi, et al., "Clinical and Immunological Assessment of Asymptomatic SARS-CoV-2 Infections," *Nature Medicine* 26, (June 18, 2020): 1200–1204.

[246] Arthur W. D. Edridge et al., "Coronavirus Protective Immunity is Short-lasting," *medRXiv*, (June 16, 2020).

[247] See Stephen Burgess et al., "Are We Underestimating Seroprevalence of SARS-CoV-2?" *BMJ*, (September 3, 2020); Ross Clark, "We May Be Closer to Herd Immunity than Previously Thought," *Spectator*, (September 3, 2020.

with asymptomatic or mild COVID-19.[248] To simplify somewhat, T cells are a type of white blood cell that recognizes and fights virus-infected cells. The study found that there is built-in T cell immunity from cross-infections of other coronaviruses such as common colds against COVID-19 as well as from exposure to SARS-CoV-2, and that such cross-reactive immunity may be present in up to half the population. Subsequently, these findings have been partially corroborated in various ways by other research teams working independently on T cells.[249] Perhaps the most promising study regarding T cells was published in July 2020. It studied T-cell responses in 36 individuals convalescing from SARS-CoV-2. The study showed that 23 patients who recovered from SARS possessed long-lasting "memory" T cells that seemed to be capable of resisting infections from SARS-CoV-2 17 years after the original SARS outbreak in 2002; that is, these T cells displayed robust immune features against SARS-CoV-2. Finally, it also detected SARS-CoV-2-specific T cells in 37 individuals with no history of SARS, COVID-19, or contact with individuals who had SARS and/or COVID-19.[250] In essence, this meant that T cells in people previously infected by other types of coronavirus last for a long time (17 years in the case of SARS) and offer a layer of immunity against SARS-CoV-2.[251] Lingering from common colds, for instance, they may be present in over half of the population at any given time and offer the probability of a persistent layer that immunizes people to various degrees.

This discovery and interpretation also offers a plausible element to explain how Sweden's mortality rate and critical cases have dropped as low as they have in spite of seeing the number of cases of infection continue steadily at around 300 per day on average since the end of June 2020. In

---

[248] Takuya Sekine, André Perez-Potti, et al., "Robust T Cell Immunity in Convalescent Individuals with Asymptomatic or Mild COVID-19," *bioRXiv*, (June 29, 2020). This study has now been accepted at *Cell* but has yet to be peer reviewed: See Takuya Sekine, André Perez-Potti, et al., "Robust T Cell Immunity in Convalescent Individuals with Asymptomatic or Mild COVID-19," *Cell*, (2020).
[249] Lauren B. Rodda, Jason Netland, et al., "Functional SARS-CoV-2-specific Immune Memory Persists after Mild COVID-19," *medRXiv*, (August 15, 2020); Matt McDonald, "An Idiot's Guide to T Cells," *Spectator USA*, (October 1, 2020).
[250] N. Le Bert et al., "SARS-CoV-2-specific T Cell Immunity in Cases of COVID-19 and SARS, and Uninfected Controls," *Nature*, 584, (2020): 457–462.
[251] See also Takuya Sekine et al., "Robust T Cell Immunity in Convalescent Individuals with Asymptomatic or Mild COVID-19," *Cell*, (preprint) (August 11, 2020).

other words, having a 15 to 20 per cent SARS-CoV-2 infection rate, added to what may have been preceding immunities from T cells, adds immunities to nearly two-thirds of the population.[252] The extent to which there may remain roughly one-third of the Swedish population vulnerable to infection in various degrees, means that there could still be a second wave of infection spike akin to what we are currently seeing in Spain, France, the U.K., Canada, and several other places. But if two-thirds already enjoy some immunity, amounting to achieving herd immunity, the intensity of whatever second wave arrives will most likely not be as strong as elsewhere in countries where the lockdowns have kept the contagion from spreading to the population without immunities. In other words, unlike antibodies, which prevent infections, T cells may help prevent people from getting sick, which is nearly as significant.

Beside the fear of nascent second waves, a few places in the world such as Brazil and India are still in the midst of the first wave. As long as the contagion continues in many other places around the world where the results are bound to be more deadly than in the more developed countries, the danger of virus reappearance in post-lockdown countries does not disappear. The possibility of renewed waves of infection and concomitant re-lockdown panics are just what the Swedish leadership meant to avoid by refraining from hard suppressive strategies.

The number of dead notwithstanding, consider again the death rates among the elderly and those most at risk, to raise one further question: learning from the mistakes made so far, would resources be better invested in the future by continuing to protect people in vulnerable categories than locking down everyone as though everyone were equally at risk? Studies have now shown clearly that children, who have more abundant T cells than adults, are the least susceptible to catching and spreading the virus, with risks so low it makes no sense to continue to oppose the re-opening of schools. If the discoveries in the multiple T-cell research were verified, the lockdown panic would have been entirely unnecessary.

Notwithstanding earlier castigations of the Swedes, it is worth pointing out that the WHO has now identified them as a likely model for countries to emulate as they emerge from lockdowns. This may be as close to an endorsement as Sweden is going to get in the foreseeable future. The

---

[252] See Ross Clark, "Is COVID Herd Immunity Closer than We Think?" *Spectator*, (June 30, 2020).

bureaucrats in this United Nations organ seem to be slowly walking themselves back from the harsh criticisms they had previously directed at Sweden. They are, therefore, tacitly endorsing the logic of the Swedish mitigating strategy. In April 2020, for example, one of the WHO's top emergency experts, Mike Ryan, praised Sweden for a public policy rooted in its people's trust, decried the cartoonish portrayal of the Swedish strategy as having done nothing to protect its people, and suggested nations would want to consider the Swedish strategy as a way to exit the lockdowns.[253] In early May, political scientist Richard Florida, a professor at the University of Toronto School of Cities, advised Toronto to adopt a version of the Swedish mitigating model as a way to exit the lockdown: "But we can borrow and learn from Sweden's intentional strategy for keeping key parts of its society open and economy up-and-running in the face of the COVID-19 pandemic."[254] The red-alert rules for Quebec in early October 2020 to deal with the resurgence of infections in some areas possess plenty of draconian features, such as closing theatres, bars, and restaurants, reducing people's mobility, regulating private human interactions, and threatening significant fines and arrests, but they did keep schools and many businesses open. Similarly, they are more discriminating and sensitive to geography as they apply for a limited time — 28 days — to the specific areas affected by resurging cases and not to the entire province. These new directives fall short of the original lockdown regime that Quebec initially adopted in March but are not the same as the Swedish mitigating model.[255]

Indirectly, even Tam has also partially endorsed the Swedish mitigating strategy. The Canadian Press reported in August that Tam, still heavily relying on alarming statistical models, was concerned about the advent of a second wave in the fall that would be "worse" than what we have seen in Canada so far. Tam was worried that at its peak, it "could overwhelm

---

[253] See Jackie Salo, "WHO Lauds Lockdown-ignoring Sweden as a 'Model' for Countries Going Forward," *New York Post*, (April 28, 2020).

[254] Richard Florida, "What Toronto Can Learn from Sweden's Coronavirus Strategy," *Toronto Star*, (May 5, 2020).

[255] Amy Luft and Daniel J. Rowe, "Red Alert: Private Gatherings Banned as Bars, Eat-in Dining Close in Three Quebec Regions," CTV News (Montreal), (September 27, 2020); and Isaac Olson, Benjamin Shingler, and Franca G. Mignacca, "Quebec Tightening COVID-19 Restrictions as 3 Regions Put on Red Alert," CBC News, (September 28, 2020).

health systems in different parts of the country." How this particular worry differs from her first round of worries, also sparked by a similar round of modelling, is not clear in the report. The first wave did not overwhelm the health systems, even if it may have strained them in some individual places in Laurentian Canada but let us recall that the lockdown was put into place to avoid that eventuality. Tam also declared, almost as if to reassure us about her news, that "Canada is better prepared than it was when the pandemic hit ... this spring." A month later, Ford commented on a second wave, announcing new restrictions to attempt containing a surge of cases in his province: "We know that we are in the second wave and we know that it will be worse than the first wave. But what we don't know yet is how bad the second wave will be."[256] The premier did not say how he knew the second wave would be worse. He just knew.

That Canada is better prepared now even though its top health official remains worried about the health system being overwhelmed does not fill one with confidence that any crucial lessons have been learned. Yet, for all her fear that what is coming is going to be worse, Tam made no mention of returning to a lockdown state yet, which is a tacit acknowledgment that the lockdown was not effective and it is not sustainable. David Williams, the chief medical officer for Ontario, was even more explicit: "Lockdowns have been shown not to eliminate the virus," he said. True, they only slow the spread (and "flatten the curve") but "this only lasts as long as the lockdown lasts" (*National Post*, October 1, 2020).[257] As we saw, these were key aspects for the Swedes' mitigating strategy. Furthermore, Tam's recent recognition that the SARS-CoV-2 virus will be among us for a few years is a validation of the initial level-headed Swedish thinking that drove that country's strategy away from a country-wide lockdown. Tam claims to be "over-preparing beyond what Canada had for the previous wave."[258] And while she has not announced that future lockdowns are out of the

---

[256] Quoted in Sean Davidson, "Ontario Tightens Visitor Policies at Some Long-term Care Homes as Second Wave Hits," CTV News, (September 29, 2020).

[257] This relatively clear remark by Williams was not, unfortunately, typical of his pronouncements. See Chris Selley, "Public Health Communications in Meltdown," *National Post*, (October 6, 2020).

[258] We may recall how seemingly simple directives were stated and reversed, at times within the day, regarding the discussion above about masks, border closures, the handling (or absence thereof) of travelers at airports, and the large donation of equipment to China leaving Canadian front-line medical workers short of crucial supplies to fight the virus, and so on.

question, she does seem to have pivoted from quarantining an entire society to quarantines for the infected. Musing about "another method to stop large outbreaks," she said, "is to ensure that people infected can be identified and quarantined as soon as possible." No one in government seems to be worried about the stigma of identifying citizens, or even the more worrying question about what it will take for and from the state to ensure that those "infected" are properly identified and "quarantined." Does she mean rounded up? Tam may not envisage a lockdown, but a mitigating approach with a rather draconian face for the next round.[259]

There is evidence that enthusiasm for lockdowns began eroding among top experts. Included among such experts is David Nabarro, who is one of six WHO special envoys for COVID-19 appointed in February 2020. In early October, Nabarro urged political leaders to "stop using lockdowns as a primary means to control the virus." In a short piece entitled "Reflections about the Middle Path," promoted on his personal Twitter account on October 8, Nabarro condemned those who let the "virus run wild" and took distance from lockdowns. Jumping to the middle, he said: "Too many restrictions damage people's livelihoods and provoke resentment."[260] Nabarro is director of the Imperial College Institute of Global Health at the Imperial College London and is director of 4SD. More than the endorsement of a mitigating middle way, the recognition that lockdowns are damaging on various levels, without ever mentioning it by name, recognizes that the Swedish approach was better than the alternatives.

One of the basic things that Sweden's mitigation strategy exposed about lockdowns is that they are a choice. SARS-CoV-2 is not the cause of the lockdowns, though that is claimed often enough. SARS-CoV-2 is the direct cause only of the sickness we now call COVID-19. The lockdowns are the direct result of panic-driven reactions by public officials and decision-makers. Lockdowns are policy choices. The effects, particularly the economic effects, which tend to be among the most immediately experienced ones, result from decisions made by governments and their agents. This is a fundamental fact that some governments have avoided acknowledging. To acknowledge a specific policy choice is to admit that governments have generated and largely contributed to the ensuing

---

[259] Canadian Press, "Expected Peak of COVID-19 Outbreak in Canada this Fall," *Globe and Mail*, (August 14, 2020).

[260] David Nabarro, "Reflections about the Middle Path," *4SD*, n.d.

recessions, the job losses, and shuttered businesses. Governments are accountable for their decisions in democracies. Instead, we hear constantly, even from sources that should know better, that the economic "devastation [is] caused by the COVID-19 pandemic."[261]

Lockdown enthusiasts are fond of saying that they have saved lives, as we saw with Ardern's declarations above, and are extremely proud of having done so, almost as if to signal that those who chose differing strategies were attempting to do the contrary. Apart from the spurious logic discussed above, the actual "excess deaths" data now show in some situations the lockdowns have contributed to more deaths than has the virus, even in circumstances where the virus was particularly lethal. Similarly, the heroics of saving lives, when predicated on the panic-inducing models, fall short of heroic because the models were and continue to be consistently wrong. One cannot have it both ways. If judged by the models, Swedes have also saved tens of thousands of lives, some 90,000 if we follow the Fergusonian model.

The bottom line is that in a pandemic contagion, however mild it seems, there are some unavoidable realities of which our culture seems to have lost sight: contagions, much like wars, bring death and suffering. Medical workers will save some lives and mitigate suffering, but medical workers cannot change the fundamental reality either for others or for themselves. Death and suffering are part of the unavoidable cost of contagion. Pretending otherwise is a detachment from reality that leads to inherently flawed responses, whether in terms of collective health or in economic terms. Much the same way that it is too early to make final pronouncements about the medical failure of the mitigating strategy, it is also too early to make grand pronouncements about the economy. Previous experiences show that the magnitude and depth of pandemic effects on economies depend largely on how governments react to them. And now that some industrial states are beginning to lift their lockdown restrictions and Sweden has come to the end of the initial infection wave, economic indicators start to point in directions that allow us to make some preliminary observations.

What some persons expected to be a superior performance by the Swedish economy compared to lockdown states has not materialized.

---

[261] Canadian Press, "C.D. Howe Says Canada has Entered a Recession due to COVID-19 Impact," Bloomberg, (May 1, 2020).

Early government statistics and experts noted that Sweden's economy has suffered as much as other European states. Similarly, projections for the aftermath of COVID-19 put Sweden's economic contractions occurring at rates comparable to those of lockdown countries with equivalent numbers of bankruptcies, job losses, and damage to markets, and supply chains. The question, considering again the apocalyptic predictions for Sweden, is why its results were not worse by orders of magnitude than in states that ordered national lockdowns.

The Swedish economy could not have been unaffected when all its neighbours and major trading partners near and far closed their borders and locked down their economies.[262] In addition, while the state did not issue orders for businesses to close down or send police to enforce such orders, Swedish business activity contracted as a result of social distancing recommendations and of a good portion of the population voluntarily staying home from work. Preliminary data show that Swedes stayed home from work just as much as, and in some cases more than, neighbouring countries with suppressive requirements.[263] But so far, the economic slowdown and the contraction of the Swedish economy at a rate of 8.6 percent in the second quarter of this year is, in relation to the previous quarter, not as pronounced as that of some of its neighbours and important trading partners in Europe and abroad. Sweden's unemployment rate climbed two points from pre-COVID-19 levels to 9.4 percent by June 2020. The EU's unemployment rate barely moved from 7.2 percent in February to 7.4 percent in June because of Europe's "furlough" scheme, which provided salary support for over 35 million people. Sweden's own scheme of economic support to businesses also did not consider the employment numbers. However, Juranek and colleagues have compared aggregated unemployment and furlough weekly data for the first 21 weeks of the COVID-19 lockdowns for the four Scandinavian

---

[262] Sweden's immediate neighbours (Norway, Finland, and Denmark), which are among its top six ranking trade partners, represent over one-quarter of its regular trade volume: Norway: US$17 billion (10.6 percent of Sweden's total exports),Germany: $16.5 billion (10.3 percent), United States: $12.2 billion (7.6 percent), Finland: $11.3 billion (seven percent), Denmark: $11.1 billion (6.9 percent), and United Kingdom: $8.5 billion (5.3 percent). See Daniel Workman, "Sweden's Top 15 Trading Partners," *World's Top Exports*, (March 1, 2020).

[263] See Lise M. Helsingen et al., "Trust, Threats, and Consequences of the COVID-19 Pandemic in Norway and Sweden – a Comparative Survey," *medRXiv* preprint, (May 20, 2020).

states, Norway, Sweden, Denmark, and Finland.[264] They observed that Sweden was the least affected labour market of the four countries: the lockdowns of Norway and Denmark had the largest impact on the labour markets, followed by Finland and Sweden last. In another recent study, Berkeley economists established a positive correlation between stay-at-home orders in American states and cumulative unemployment insurance claims, both measured through April 4, 2020. In places where governments issued such orders, the applications for benefits surged intensely in tandem. They also recorded a link between the stay-at-home orders and the drop in retail movement in the United States.[265] This does not mean that states that did not issue stay-at-home orders have not suffered economically from the pandemic, nor does it mean that lifting the stay-at-home orders will immediately fix the unemployment surge. Levels of employment and unemployment drive consumer spending. Early data from Denmark in the initial days of the lockdown show a drop in consumer spending by as much as 25 percent.[266] There are significant numbers of speculative studies relying on models to ascertain how the pandemic does or will affect the economy.[267] We will have to wait for the calculation of actual data and other indicators such as the incurred debt per capita ratio and the rate of economic recovery for a better picture.

The *Washington Post* reported that "the Eurozone's gross domestic product fell 40.3% on an annual basis … the equivalent to a 12.1% decline from the previous quarter."[268] So, collectively, the EU decline is about one-third deeper than Sweden's. None of this should be a surprise to anyone by now. As the BBC's economic correspondent, Andrew Walker, put it: "Lockdowns earlier in the pandemic were draconian and … many people

---

[264] Steffen Juranek, Jörg Paetzold, at al., "Labour Market Effects of COVID-19: Sweden and its Scandinavian Neighbours," *VOXeu*, (September 12, 2020).

[265] ChaeWon Baek, Peter B. McCrory, et al., "Unemployment Effects of Stay-at-home Orders: Evidence from High-frequency Claims Data," *VOXeu*, (April 30, 2020).

[266] A. Andersen, E. Hansen, N. Johannesen, and A. Sheridan, "Consumer Responses to the COVID-19 Crisis: Evidence from Bank Account Transaction Data," *Covid Economics* 7, (2020): 88–114.

[267] See, for example,, Simon Wren-Lewis, "The Economic Effects of a Pandemic," in Richard Baldwin and Beatrice Weder di Mauro, eds., *Economics in the Time of COVID-19*, (London: Centre for Economic Policy Research Press, 2020).

[268] Tom Fairless, "Europe Plunges into Recession as Economy Suffers Record Contraction," *Washington Post*, (July 31, 2020).

have been wary of exposing themselves to the risk of infection. The result was some extraordinary declines in economic activity."[269] One can't consistently scare people half to death for several weeks and then expect that all will be well the following month.

As compared to Canada, Sweden was in a much better economic position before the crisis, and all things being equal, will likely better weather the economic impact, provided Europe recovers at a similar rate. One reason is Canada's dependency on the American recovery. Besides, Sweden's economic fundamentals are stronger than Canada's. Its debt to GDP ratio before COVID-19 was 56 percent compared to Canada's 108 percent. Sweden's general government financial wealth was 28 percent as opposed to Canada's -35 percent for 2019. Canada's investment prospects are also weaker. Swedish household savings on the average for 2019 were 17.64 percent while Canada's were 2.13 percent, 17 times lower. Household savings, according to the OECD, were already projected to continue lowering for Canada and trending upward for Sweden in the 2021 forecast.[270]

---

[269] Andrew Walker, "Eurozone Suffers Deepest Contraction on Record," BBC News, (July 31, 2020).
[270] See Organization for Economic Co-operation and Development, https:/data.oece.org.

Political Fallout in Canada

The economic cost of forcing nearly 3.3 million Canadians into unemployment by May 2020 is enormous and has yet to be tallied in full. While individuals and companies were able to receive some form of help from their governments, many businesses will not be able to rebound from their losses and many who do will not long survive. The corrupting effect of subsidy is also being felt outside of the economic sphere, with many now pushing for the lockdown to continue, either because they live in fear of being infected by the virus or because the subsidies have made it more desirable to remain home than to work. As Félix Leclerc wrote in the 1950s: "The best way to kill a man is to pay him to do nothing."

By March 2020, the Canadian economy had shrunk 7.2 percent, but the pandemic shutdowns did not begin until the middle of the month. April saw the economy contract by 11.6 percent, the deepest drop on record. About one-third of the workforce remains under-utilized by the fall 2020, either as a result of the highest unemployment since the 2009 recession, or as a result of roughly a million individuals ceasing to look for work. Across most of the private sector, economic activity shrunk in record amounts. In March, manufacturing fell 22.5 percent, construction fell 22.9 percent, retail and hospitality fell 42 percent, and transportation fell a shocking 93.7 percent.[271] In Atlantic Canada, for example, the governments of Newfoundland and Labrador, Prince Edward Island, Nova Scotia, and New Brunswick have opted for establishing a regional "bubble." The rules allow for interregional travel but make it difficult for people "from away" to enter and exit. As a result, airports lost 92 percent of their summer traffic. The bubble decision caused the region to lose over five million visitors, forgoing the better part of $140 million in revenue for their

---

[271] Guy Gellatly and Carter McCormack, "Recent Developments in the Canadian Economy, 2020: COVID-19, Second Edition," StatsCan, (June 24, 2020).

airports.[272] Figures for Canada show that between April and June, the annualized GDP dropped by 38.7 percent. By the summer, the deficit was 16 percent of GDP, the largest in the G7.

Government subsidies to individuals and businesses constitute the kind of help that hurts. It hurts people psychologically and economically, but the monetary subsidies most people received fell short of their effective losses, both for businesses and for individuals. These losses, again, were policy-induced, and their direct effects will be felt for years to come.[273] Moreover, the government of Canada paid its citizens directly, whereas the Americans relied on businesses to channel money to citizens, which had the effect of maintaining the monetary link between businesses and employees. The difference was significant inasmuch as simple direct payments to Canadian citizens were offset by complex payment deferrals and loans to companies. Philip Cross suggested the approach chosen expressed the typical suspicion of recent Liberal governments towards business in Canada. This obviously contrasted with the American attitude, but more importantly, it ensured that the reopening of the Canadian economy would take longer and would be accompanied by much greater hesitation than in the U.S.[274]

The Conference Board of Canada came to a related conclusion about the state of the economy: "What we've come to realize is the economy will be operating well below (pre-pandemic) levels" for some time.[275] In short, things are worse than originally expected. In addition, the massive debt that the provinces and federal government have taken on as a result of the decision to lock down will weigh heavy over the next couple of generations. No expression could better describe the disconnect between the dire effects of policy decisions and the economic realities Canadians will have to face in the future than the prime minister's belief that his government had relieved the burdens of economic responsibility from

---

[272] Canadian Press, "Airports in Atlantic Canada Estimate 92% Drop in Spring and Summer Travel," CBC News, (September 22, 2020).

[273] Guy Gellatly and Carter McCormack, "Recent Developments in the Canadian Economy."

[274] Philip Cross, "What Canada's Response to the Pandemic says about Canada – and the US," *Inside Policy*, (September 2020): 11–12.

[275] Victor Ferreira, "Pandemic's Cost Worse than First Predicted, and Alberta Economy to Take Biggest Hit: Conference Board," *National Post*, (August 24, 2020).

Canadian citizens; he declared that his government had taken on massive debt so that Canadians would not have to.[276] Let us be frank: this is absurd.

In Alberta, where the authors live, and where a recession already was in place (in 2019, the Alberta economy contracted by 0.6 percent when the average growth in the country was 1.7 percent), the anticipated COVID-19 effects promise to be devastating. Making matters worse, Alberta's economy has been at the receiving end of two critical blows before and during the pandemic. A market glut of oil produced by a price war between Russia and Saudi Arabia reduced prices to levels that sent Canadian oil producers into massive cash-crunches, prompting new rounds of job losses to the province. In addition, as is well known, Alberta has been besieged for years by a federal policy embargo against development of its hydrocarbon resources. The province has for some time been economically choked by the Canadian government's application of impossible standards to projects that would never be imposed on other industries — and in some cases, are not even imposed to the same or similar industries in other provinces. Simultaneously, Ottawa, having been encouraged by eco-radicals and less-than-friendly sister provinces, has blocked efforts both to the east and west to build more capacity to send Alberta resources to market.[277] Alberta then received Edmonton's orders to lock down on March 17, 2020,[278] adding an extra layer to further cripple its economic activity.[279] Robert Roach, Alberta Treasury Branch's director of economics and research, noted that things in Alberta are currently in a "brutal" situation, pointing out that "this is going to be a year of deep recession."[280] The depth of the brutality Roach described in June is the result of the confluence of these economic and political hurdles facing the province. By mid-September, the situation in the province continued to

---

[276] Justin Trudeau commenting on a fiscal update, CTV News Montreal, (July 8, 2020).

[277] See Marco Navarro-Génie, "Stalling Frontier's Approval is the Most Likely Cabinet Decision," *Western Standard*, (February 10, 2020); and Marco Navarro-Génie, "Eco-ideologues at the Ready to Profit from Crises," *Western Standard*, (April 8, 2020).

[278] Alberta Government, Order in Council 80/20: Health — Declaring a State of Public Health Emergency, (March 17, 2020).

[279] Marco Navarro-Génie, "Three Elements Converge into a Perfect Economic Storm for Alberta," *Western Standard*, (March 25, 2020).

[280] Wallis Snowdon, "COVID-19 Will Make 2020 Even Worse, Economist Says," CBC News, (June 3, 2020).

deteriorate because of the consequences of the lockdown, which were more severe than in the rest of the country. "The lingering effect of COVID-19 continues to be felt harder in Alberta," writes veteran Alberta journalist Bill Kaufmann, "with 53 percent of residents' financial lives still disrupted," whereas the equivalent figure for the rest of the country is 10 points lower. Similarly, 20 percent of Albertans are struggling with reduced work hours, where the equivalent is 15 percent in the rest of the country.[281]

According to the Conference Board, the Alberta economy is expected to contract 11.3 percent this year, whereas Ontario and Quebec contractions are expected to be 7.6 and 7.2 percent, respectively. Making the point that lockdowns hurt economies, the Conference Board signaled that in spite of Quebec having the worst record of COVID-19 deaths in the country, "the damage to its economy would have been worse if not for the government's decision to begin the reopening process earlier than others."[282] A full economic evaluation will have to wait, especially in light of probable renewed lockdowns, but it seems clear that government policy, in addition to making Canadians less healthy, has also made us poorer. At the same time, the central government has advanced a self-serving, power-increasing political agenda shielded from parliamentary oversight.

A careful review of reporting on the COVID-19 pandemic and its ensuing panic will indicate the strong ideological component to the responses to it. On a right-left axis, one can predict with a significant deal of accuracy on which side of the argument an individual is going to fall on the question of masks, vaccines, "social distancing," and the like. That is curious because, as we have seen regarding the efficacy of masks, for example, the science involved is both ambiguous and technical, which is to say not a matter of political opinion or voter inclinations. This is especially true in North America, though Europe has not escaped this strange problem. For example, when the government of Denmark initially shunned the use of masks as it tried to transition out of the lockdown, it cited the lack of robust evidence that mask use prevents the spread of COVID-19 and mentioned that the scientific literature showed the use of masks in some cases might even contribute to the spread. One of the

---

[281] Bill Kaufmann, "More than Half of Albertans Still Face Job Loss, Reduced Pay and Hours due to Pandemic: Survey," *Edmonton Journal*, (September 17, 2020).
[282] Quoted in Victor Ferreira, "Pandemic's Cost Worse than First Predicted, and Alberta Economy to Take Biggest Hit."

reactions to what is simply scientific evidence compared the Danish government to Trump's administration.

Rahm Emmanuel echoed Sir Winston Churchill's dictum: "Never let a good crisis go to waste," in formulating the response of the Obama administration to the recession of 2008. The COVID-19 pandemic certainly presented a splendid policy opportunity to segments of the knowledge class, as we pointed out above. One of the first political byproducts was a massive increase in their power. But clearly visible as well were federal and provincial efforts to increase the power of government.

One hallmark of a healthy liberal democracy lies in the strength and performance of the political opposition. The Trudeau government is a minority government. By nature, minority governments have a larger opposition and are less powerful than those governing with majorities. Minority governments must actively seek agreement with other parliamentary parties and so-called stakeholders in order to get anything done. Finding agreement is typically difficult and requires political skill; that is, good judgment and the ability to work well with others. It also requires sufficient maturity and humility to recognize that the ideas and political positions of others, however opposite to one's own, have some validity. If nothing else, they are valid because the views of opposition MPs represent the views of those who elected them in various parts of the country. Dismissing the views advanced by their representatives is to dismiss those who sent them there.

The initial instinct of the Trudeau government's effort to take advantage of the COVID-19 pandemic panic was to transfer power from the House of Commons to the Finance minister. It was certainly one way to deal with the opposition. Bill C-13 aimed to give then-Finance minister Bill Morneau nearly unlimited power to tax, spend, borrow, and lend until the end of 2021, which at the time was 21 months away. For comparison, in 1939, the United Kingdom delegated legislative authority to the war cabinet — except regarding taxation. The Trudeau government's ambitions were subsequently reduced to six months of essentially unlimited power during which time Parliament was turned into a virtual assembly. Conrad Black may have been over-generous when he described what seemed to be an obvious power grab as "more an act of panic than of usurpation" (*National Post*, March 28, 2020). We find neither alternative comforting.

Rex Murphy, also writing in the *National Post* (July11, 2020) summarized the government's strategy: "COVID-19 has been the Trudeau government's umbrella and shield. Government has exploited the cover it has given them — perfect freedom to completely ignore the customs and procedures of Parliamentary democracy. Under that meretricious licence it has swollen the deficit to $343 billion and the national debt to $1.2 *trillion*."

Without parliamentary scrutiny the executive has no compelling reason to be prudent or even responsible. As Christian Leuprecht observed: "A democracy should reciprocate unprecedented restrictions on individual freedoms and unprecedented levels of spending with unprecedented levels of debate and scrutiny."[283] Instead, the Trudeau Liberals, with the help of the NDP, imposed the opposite: limit debate, increase spending, and abjure responsibility. In effect, policy became whatever the prime minister feels good about. Canada's way of dealing with COVID-19 was as far removed from Sweden's as it is possible to get. We can take cold comfort in the knowledge that other countries have made similar attempts to increase state power. In short, the government of Canada has attempted to bypass the will of Canadians who may have returned Trudeau to office, but at the head of a minority government with, at 22 percent of the popular vote, the smallest percentage of popular support in Canadian history. Canada's federal government does not have the monopoly on this kind of action to increase its power. Governments around the world — dictatorships and liberal democracies — sometimes barely days into the pandemic, made similar attempts at increasing their share of power. [284]

The *Emergencies Act* did contemplate the transfer of enormous authority to the federal government during emergencies, including powers that belonged exclusively to provincial jurisdictions, but only for renewable periods of 90 days. [285] But no previous Parliament considering emergencies had contemplated relieving the House of Commons of one of its most significant features, the supervision of executive fiscal powers. There was nothing in the present situation that was so radically unusual to warrant

---

[283] Christian Leuprecht, "Decision to Suspend Parliament during the Pandemic was Wrong," *Inside Policy*, (June 2020).

[284] See, for example, "Coronavirus: Is Pandemic Being Used for Power Grab in Europe?" BBC News, (April 17, 2020).

[285] Government of Canada, The *Emergencies Act* (1985). https://laws-lois.justice.gc.ca/eng/acts/e-4.5/page-1.html.

providing the government with an accountability furlough. There was nothing so different about this government that Canadians should trust them seven times more than they have thought to trust previous governments under the *Emergencies Act*. What the Trudeau government wanted to do is not contemplated by the *Emergencies Act* because it was so obviously unconstitutional.

One need not believe that Trudeau intended to turn Canada into a banana republic, though what Guilherme France, research director for Transparency International in Brazil, said of that country clearly could be said of Trudeau's Canada: "The pandemic allowed governments to spend significant resources very quickly while internal controls were relaxed due to the emergency. It ended up creating the perfect storm for corruption" (*National Post*, September 26, 2020). By early March at the latest, it was clear that the Trudeau Liberals meant to rule without annoying limitations that get in the way of what Trudeau perceives to be his good intentions and virtuous desires. The move simply sought to take advantage of a crisis to gain self-serving political convenience. It would have insulated the minority government from all possibility of losing a vote on a money bill, turning a minority government into an invincible super-minority. It would have entirely freed the Liberal government from the distractions of opposition, allowing them to govern in a minority without having to satisfy the House on financial matters, and without having to make the compromises that are typical of normal politics. To state the obvious: government without limitations is very rarely good government. The absence of restraint almost always opens great avenues for abusing power. Moreover, this government had already proved itself reluctant to follow rules and respect the law. Its ethical record has been terrible.

Scarcely a month into the lockdown, in another bid to use the pandemic as an opportunity to augment state power and diminish the individual liberties of Canadian citizens, the federal cabinet discussed introducing legislation to regulate information related to the pandemic. This was a way, they argued, to protect the public from the dissemination of false or erroneous information, online fake news, and other varieties of misinformation and disinformation. The minister in charge of the file, and president of the Privy Council, Dominic LeBlanc, revealed that cabinet was considering "legislation to make it an offence to knowingly spread misinformation that could harm people."[286] New laws were needed during the pandemic, he claimed, along with new rules about mischief on social media. "Extraordinary times require extraordinary measures and it is about protecting the public." It had nothing to do with limiting freedom of speech, he said.[287] Even if that were true or even plausible, the most egregiously stupid aspect of the proposal was that federal government officials had for months disseminated false information and baseless opinions on government social media channels and on mainstream sources about the coronavirus, China, the WHO, the effectiveness of wearing masks, the success of lockdowns, and the closure of borders, among other things.

The consequences could be foreseen easily enough: a decline in citizens' trust in government and official sources of information precisely because they were inconsistent and often in conflict with non-government sources. This may not have been a government-made problem, to be sure, but governments were unprepared, were having trouble inspiring confidence in their own citizens, and were contributing to the lack of trust with their self-contradictory communications. LeBlanc added that government control of speech over social media was in his mandate letters dating back to the previous fall. Raising such a legalistic issue during the initial days of the COVID-19 crisis seemed like exploiting an opportunity to ram through legislation and prevent opponents and critics of the lockdown and of many of its accompanying policies to be questioned publicly. Likewise, in Alberta, the government said it "needed" laws to regulate prices in the market in the middle of the toilet paper crisis that so bizarrely characterized the beginning of the COVID-19 panic around the world. Ontario and British Columbia did likewise.

Given the attempted power grab and what later ensued with the WE Charity scandal, it is not difficult to see that the cabinet wanted to push its policy agenda as quickly as it could by capitalizing on the pandemic days, during which time Parliament was effectively dormant and government encountered the least amount of political opposition. The federal government exclusively retained the WE Charity organization, without an open bidding process, to deliver a youth program worth over $900 million

---

[286] Elizabeth Thompson, "Federal Government Open to New Law to Fight Pandemic Misinformation," CBC News, (April 15, 2020).
[287] Terry Haig, "Laws to Fight COVID-19 Misinformation are in the Political Hopper," Radio Canada International, (April 15, 2020).

that would leave the WE Charity with $43.53 million in earnings, according to the contract. The prime minister justified the sole-source contract by claiming that no one else in the country, no other organization, including the federal civil service, could do the work as required. The prime minister made the announcement, outlining that the decision followed a discussion that ended with his cabinet's approval. The WE Charity withdrew from the contract several days later, when it was revealed that key ministers, including the ministers of Finance and Energy, and the prime minister, all had had dealings with and personal links to the organization. Two of the Finance minister's children were involved with the organization; in Trudeau's case, the organization has paid members of his family as much as half a million dollars in fees and expenses for their participation in WE Charity events. Later, it was revealed that Morneau had even been treated to a $41,366 vacation to South America and Africa paid for by a branch of WE Charity. He then abruptly resigned his post and his seat in the Commons on August 17, but Ethics Commissioner Mario Dion continued his investigations into Morneau's and Trudeau's dealings with the WE Charity.[288]

The WE Charity scandal presents yet another government attempt at circumventing laws, policies and regulations, bypassing the civil service under the guise of addressing a fabricated need during the COVID-19 crisis, in order to prioritize Trudeau's desire to pay back those who rewarded members of his family or those close to him and his party. The SNC-Lavalin scandal of a year earlier bears the identical government modus operandi. The political significance of this latest scandal, besides claiming a senior cabinet minister, may have further consequences for the government. Losing a Finance minister in the midst of the greatest financial crisis the country has seen since the Great Depression is a major political event, but the scandal may yet yield criminal charges, and could cost the prime minister his job. However, it unfolds, it has brought a crisis to the government in the exercise of decisions made ostensibly to deal with COVID-19 crisis fallout.

---

[288] Peter Zimonjic and David Cochrane, "Bill Morneau Resigns as Finance Minister and MP, Will Seek to Lead OECD," CBC News, (August 17, 2020). Neither the minister resigning nor the statement made by the prime minister alluded to the scandal. See PMO, "Statement by the Prime Minister on Minister Bill Morneau's Resignation," (August 17, 2020).

In the midst of all this rather tedious corruption-as-usual that has become one of the defining characteristics of recent Liberal governments, we can count on Quebec politicians to provide comic relief. Not quite as absurd, perhaps, as the crafting of a $1.5 million jewel-encrusted mask (*National Post*, August 13, 2020), the sensitivities of Quebec politicians to the slighting of their version of the French language remained robust. In May 2020, Sonia LeBel, Quebec's minister for Relations with Canada and Francophones, complained that Health Canada allowed the importation and use of disinfectants and antiseptics without French labelling. Marni Soupcoff took her measure: "Better to be infected by SARS-CoV-2 than by English." Bloc Québécois House Leader Alain Therrien called Ottawa's move a Trojan horse as well as a Pandora's box, showing an imperfect command of classical images (*National Post*, May 1, 2020).

When the federal government announced its aid package, the premiers, of course, said it was not enough. Quebec in particular advanced an interesting argument. Premier François Legault said Quebec was not interested in any conditions: "I was very clear that we want part of the $14 billion, but we don't want it to be conditional to anything." How big a part? Well, "we know that Quebec had more cases than the rest of the country, so we think we should receive more than the 23 percent our population represents in Canada (*National Post*, June 6, 2020). Of course.

As a final example of a moral panic in action, consider the snitch. Within days of locking down and before March was over, all provinces established "snitch lines" — dedicated phone lines that citizens could use to report on other citizens who, in the informant's opinion, failed to comply with lockdown rules. Already existing platforms such as phone lines kicked into high gear, and in Newfoundland and Labrador and in Alberta, additional online portals would receive complaints. The move seemed innocently born out of fear and concern, but it was fraught with potential dangers and adverse consequences for the political community and for individuals. In the same way that "fear isn't healthy for science," as epidemiologist Ioannidis pointed out, fear is a terrible guide to public policy and legislation, and a highly toxic element for governments to mix into the private interactions of the members of a community.[289] News outlets reported that thousands of calls and messages had been placed to

---

[289] Quoted in Saurabh Jha, "John Ioannidis Explains His COVID Views," *Medscape*, (July 15, 2020).

governments through platforms created for these purposes. In Alberta alone, between March and August, close to 20,000 complaints were launched in a province with 15,957 confirmed COVID-19 cases by September 16. That there were more citizen-on-citizen complaints than there were actual infection cases in that time frame indicated an epidemic of panic among Albertans,[290] with likely equivalences in the rest of the country.

Leading the road paved with good intentions, Maryse Zeidler of CBC described people inclined to denounce their own neighbours as "citizen groups that help with law enforcement." This is meant to dress up snitching as community-minded action.[291] Zeidler apparently thought that informing on one's neighbours helps to save lives. Informants may see themselves as patriots of sorts, akin to those who would inform on spies during wartime: resistance fighters rather than agents of conformity. An April 1 *Medicine Hat News* headline, making no argument and offering nothing more than an official communiqué from the Alberta government on rules regarding COVID-19 and on how to inform on others, proudly summarized the sentiment: "It's Not Snitching If It Saves Lives: Ways to Report COVID-19 Rule-breakers." Written under the byline of Gillian Slade, the piece looked like a news article.[292] By including about a dozen words of their own, the journalists in Medicine Hat tried to normalize and praise community informants. Given the date of publication, perhaps the editor had a sense of humour. In addition, because public policies always have unintended consequences, it has been reported that plenty of calls were provoked by such trivial things as complaints about the length of the lineups at the grocery stores.[293] A couple of weeks earlier, the complaints might have been about toilet paper. Analytically, there may be a clear line between informant and vigilante. Discounting mischief, an informant reports when others may be doing something that the person informing finds improper, inappropriate, or illegal. The vigilante makes a similar

---

[290] Bill Kaufmann, "AHS Receives Nearly 20,000 Complaints of Albertans Not Following COVID-19 Guidelines," *Calgary Herald*, (August 22, 2020).

[291] Maryse Zeidler, "The Pleasure and Peril of Snitching on Your Neighbours during a Pandemic," CBC, (April 26, 2020).

[292] Gillian Slade, "It's Not Snitching If It Saves Lives: Ways to Report COVID-19 Rule breakers," *Medicine Hat News*, (April 1, 2020).

[293] Gillian Slade, "It's Not Snitching If It Saves Lives: Ways to Report COVID-19 Rule breakers," *Medicine Hat News*, (April 1, 2020).

moral call and decides to do something about it and becomes more involved as he perceives himself to be an enforcer or as someone assisting law enforcement. The point, however, is that snitch lines empower both.

Informants who shared their opinions with reporters expressed pride and self-satisfaction as well as indignation and fear. "I was appalled and scared," a British Columbia female informant, who is an asthmatic cancer survivor, told CBC. She denounced the presence of nine people in a restricted park, including children, who in her opinion were not following social distancing rules.[294] Children seem naturally to dislike wearing masks and to avoid distancing rules. The younger they are the worse it is, as we saw in the case of the toddler travelling on WestJet, mentioned earlier. Perhaps less well intended, one citizen gleefully threatened another outside of a Walmart store when he noticed someone had the sniffles and was using a paper tissue to blow his nose. He took photos of the allegedly infectious person and of his vehicle's licence plate before threatening to call the police. "I [felt] great. I didn't have to wait for the police ... I got the fear right into this guy,"[295] he said. The word "bully" never appeared in the news media report.

There have been a few reported cases in which vigilante types have crossed the line with dangerous or lethal consequences during the high-anxiety early days of the pandemic. In Pennsylvania, two men traded gunfire in a parking lot in broad daylight after one individual scolded the other for coughing in public without covering his mouth.[296] At around the same time in New York City, a woman was charged with homicide for hitting an elderly woman in a Brooklyn hospital. The victim fell after being struck for what the aggressive younger female thought was a violation of mandated distancing.[297]

The benign interpretation of citizens turned state informants is based on the idea that the action to inform and denounce wrongdoing is a good in itself because it aims at some notion of the common good. Two Alberta

---

[294] Cited in Maryse Zeidler, "The Pleasure and Peril."

[295] Quoted by staff in "Should We Tattle on People Breaking the COVID-19 Rules? 2 Differing Sides Debate," CBC Calgary, (April 23, 2020).

[296] Crispin Havener, "Man 'Coughing and Not Covering' Led to Shots Fired at Johnstown Sheetz," WJAC, (March 31, 2020).

[297] See Rocco Parascandola, Ellen Moynihan, and John Annese, "Brooklyn Woman, 86, Dies after She's Knocked to the Ground for Violating Coronavirus Social Distancing," New York Daily News, (March 29, 2020).

political scientists who published an essay for CBC in early April echoed the justification for unusual measures used by LeBlanc, who, as we saw, wanted to suppress "misinformation." Clothed in pseudo-scientific modelling, the authors announced there were "four kinds of people." Most importantly, there were selfish people who defied the rules and were dangerous because they shun "collective responsibility." Such persons "can ruin the hard work of public health officials" and promote questionable behaviour. Therefore, they need to be constrained for the common good.[298] Their argument supported the imposition of state power and the use of punishment, including confinement, to ensure conformity. That coercive power in the name of the collective good against conscientious objectors, dissenters, or unsuspecting minorities could be (and has historically been) misused did not enter into their argument for a moment. A similar attitude without academic pretentions was expressed by a Toronto city councillor, Stephen Holyday. Violating the traditional norm that elected officials do not comment on matters that are, or may come, before a court of law, Holyday celebrated the fact that Dylan Finlay, a Toronto jogger, received an $800 ticket for exercising in Toronto's Centennial Park during the pandemic. "If I was (sic) writing the ticket, I'd write a $5,000 ticket," Holyday said.[299]

That the collective good must come first in certain conditions is not necessarily a bad thing but suggesting that a fine more than six times the prescribed lawful punishment should be imposed on a fitness-minded citizen is simply ridiculous. A $5,000 fine would violate established law to indulge the councillor's personal feeling. So, the citizen who seeks to remain healthy (and perhaps even sane) by exercising (saving money for the collective in the process) is selfish and should be punished far beyond the requirements of the law, but the elected official who would violate the law on a whim to punish others for doing something he or she disapproved of gets his name in the news as a kind of hero who advocates the saving of lives. There are two standards here. And in much the same way, the mayor of Toronto and another city councillor a month later descended upon the masses on Trinity Bellwoods Park to shame people. Thousands of Torontonians roamed the park taking advantage of a sunny spring day

---

[298] See Melanee Thomas and Lisa Lambert, "A COVID-19 Smackdown: Why Rule Breakers Need to be Punished," CBC, (April 18, 2020).

[299] Staff, Global News, "Coronavirus: Chin-ups at West Toronto Park Earn Man $800 Fine," (April 15, 2020).

but failing to keep the mandated distance. After being photographed in violation of the same distancing rules for which he was trying to shame citizens, Mayor John Tory was forced to apologize.[300] No ticket was ever issued against His Worship. Like many other politicians during the COVID-19 pandemic, Tory thought he could violate the rules with some impunity by "unsafely" mingling with people in one Toronto park although Finlay could not exercise all by himself a month earlier in another park in the same city. The collective good is often a convenient means to exert control over the behaviour of others.

There are many other reasons than privileging collectivism that make government-encouraged citizens snitching on other citizens deplorable. While some argue that it can have a salutary effect on strengthening communities, we would argue that it does precisely the opposite by pitting people against each other. It weakens the bonds of community, fosters suspicion among neighbours, and at the same time encourages people to rely more closely on government agents rather than on their neighbours. The result leaves a locked-down individual even more isolated from their neighbours and friends, and more dependent on the state and its agents. This is precisely the least salutary situation during a pandemic, when the state is already demanding that people keep away from each other. Jen Gerson makes this point rather forcefully: "Snitch lines are an evil tool in a time of crisis because they damage the trust that we need to create resiliency in our communities." Gerson's piece, published in *Maclean's* at the end of April, described the implications of how turning neighbour against neighbour undermined community, fed panic, and sets the stage, as an authoritarian mechanism, to undermine liberal democracy in the midst of what she called the "maw of panic."

Consenting citizens, the kind desirable in liberal democracies, do not need mass coercion and state manipulation of fearful situations to exercise their civic responsibilities. Most people raised in liberal settings will only accept being bullied and pushed by their own governments temporarily, which is the reason why coercion cannot take us very far. As Tegnell said, it's not sustainable. It brings us to a fork in the road, as Gerson also points out: "We sit on a precipice, here. Either informed and consenting citizens

---

[300] Betsy Powell, "Mayor Apologizes for Breaking COVID-19 Rules at Trinity Bellwoods Park," *Toronto Star*, (May 24, 2020).

will continue to engage in social distancing to the degree to which they are able; or we are going to accept increasingly authoritarian measures of social control, demanding our governments clamp down ever more strictly until the mob clamours for the #Covidiots to be literally welded into their homes — as the Chinese authorities have done."[301]

When we look at the discussion in Quebec, her words seem prophetic. During the second week of September 2020, the government of Quebec, seeing the number of infections rise in what they saw as a "second-wave" phenomenon, considered how to clamp down on meetings and gatherings of people in private dwellings, which they considered to be the principal source of the virus's propagation. Quebec had "relaxed" its strict lockdown rules to allow as many as 10 people to gather in private homes. Seeing that there may be house parties violating this rule, authorities then considered how to get around constitutional provisions prohibiting police entering people's homes to enforce COVID-19 distancing and the 10-people rule.[302] Meanwhile, a significant operation was launched to have police presence in as many as 1,000 bars where "Police will be making sure public health guidelines are followed and handing out infractions to both businesses and clients who defy them."[303] The previous weekend, on Saturday, September 12, several thousand Quebecers marched to protest the COVID-19 regime, refusing to wear masks and demanding that the lockdown end.[304] Mainstream media reports made significant efforts to portray the demonstrations as radical and out of touch. It was not, however, the first march, nor will it likely be the last. The September protest followed protests in Montreal in August and in July 2020.[305] On September 17, the CBC published a story about a litany of direct threats to Quebec authorities and journalists on the part of "radical elements,"

---

[301] Jen Gerson, "Don't Let Coronavirus Turn us into a Nation of Snitches," *Maclean's*, (April 20, 2020).

[302] Sidhartha Banerjee, "Quebec Looking at Ways the State Can Intervene in Private Homes to Stop COVID-19," *National Post*, (September 16, 2020).

[303] Katelyn Thomas, "Quebec Public Security Minister Announces Province-wide Police Operation for the Weekend," CTV News (Montreal), (September 18, 2020).

[304] See Jonathan Montpetit and John MacFarlane, "Anti-mask Protest in Montreal Draws Large Crowd, Propelled by U.S. Conspiracy Theories," CBC News, (September 12, 2020); Sandani Hapuhennedige, "Public Health Experts Learning from Canada's Anti-Mask Protests," *CMAJ News*, (October 1, 2020).

[305] Staff, CBC News, "Thousands Rally in Downtown Montreal to Protest Quebec's Mandatory Mask Rules," (August 8, 2020).

once again supposedly propelled by unnamed conspiracy theories. While COVID-19 may have given rise to plenty of conspiracies, opposition to the lockdown is not evidence of embracing one. While there is no denying that COVID-19 has increased certain kinds of mental illness, the legitimate questioning of authority and experts, who have often been wrong or have disseminated erroneous information about the virus, is not evidence of lunacy.

There are plenty of other revealing pieces of anecdotal evidence that suggest the population that has borne the brunt of the repressive, panicked, and incompetent policies of the government of Canada has just about had enough. For example, "a poll conducted last month for Montreal's *La Presse* newspaper suggested 35 per cent of the population believe mainstream media outlets are spreading false information about COVID-19," reported CBC. Only 35 percent? There has been an increase in threats, including threats on social media, to politicians and experts. The national broadcaster reports that: "The Sûreté du Québec says it has received 300 reports since March about Quebec politicians being threatened on social media — an increase of more than 450 per cent over the same period last year."[306] To return to an earlier point: even though the federal government did not invoke the *Emergencies Act*, it nevertheless went in some respects far beyond what the act would have allowed, even in Quebec.

Police services enforced with apparent gusto the new regime regarding physical distancing, for example, though they had refused to enforce long-standing laws on road-blockading gangs just a few weeks earlier in 2020. According to one source, between March and June 2020, police in Canada issued 11,602 charges regarding violations of coronavirus regulations (not including charges laid by Quebec provincial police).[307] Police chased away parents with small children from parks, playgrounds, and pathways, and turned people away from public roads. Those who questioned or objected were fined hundreds of dollars. One Ottawa teenager was fined $700 for shooting hoops in a parking lot by himself. Others were roughly handled

---

[306] Jonathan Montpetit, "Quebec Extremists Radicalized by COVID-19 Conspiracy Theories Could Turn to Violence, Experts Warn," CBC News, (September 17, 2020).
[307] *True North Wire*, (September 2, 2020).

and carted away, even when seemingly following every rule.[308] The term Covidiots applied to those who questioned or rejected the panic and the abuses by the authorities. As Gerson expressed it a month into the Canadian lockdown, the Twitter hashtag term was "initially intended to accompany candid camera shots of callous young people gathering, it grew into a broader habit of gleefully shaming anybody displaying behaviours that were considered sane and normal only a few weeks ago."[309] All the while, hospitals went largely empty across the country, and the most vulnerable were condemned to suffer in warehouses for the elderly, producing so far over 90 percent of all deaths in Canada.

Reopening too quickly, we were told, risked losing all the sacrifices previously made. Then, nearly 12 weeks after the lockdown began, the moral panic induced by COVID-19 policy was temporarily suspended and replaced by a new expression of moral panic, this time dealing with the exaggerated racial tensions following the death of George Floyd in the United States. That event exposed schizophrenic aspects of Canadian culture and their influence on governments' behaviour during the COVID-19 lockdown. Upon one unfortunate death in a foreign country, life-saving medical measures no longer mattered so that emotive, virtue-signaling crowds (and at times mobs) could come together and demonstrate their concern. Suddenly, medical authorities did not seem concerned with large gatherings and the risks of transmission. Suddenly, venting in protest against Canadian police services was more important than saving lives from COVID-19 infection.

Politicians quickly knelt in front of the parade, ignoring laws they had just installed. No one required them to obey the rules. No one enforced what days earlier had been imposed with the enthusiasm of bullies. The personal, social, and economic sacrifices of so many, including the elderly

---

[308] Dean Bennett, "Kenney Questions Arrest of Pandemic Lockdown Protester at Alberta Legislature," Global News, (May 11, 2020). The individual in question was manhandled by Alberta Legislature sheriffs and charged under the *Public Health Act* for obstructing officers by refusing to provide identification and for participating in a public gathering of more than 15 people, even though video footage clearly shows that he was sitting by himself and keeping more than the mandated distance from everyone else.

[309] See Jen Gerson, "Don't Let Coronavirus."

we did not properly protect, may have been erased by a media-whipped, triggered crowd (to say nothing of looters). The outrage regarding the large numbers of dead among those the government claimed to be protecting with the lockdown remains absent. There were no blunt messages from politicians telling people to stay home, and ranking medical officers spoke approvingly of the protest gatherings.

Make no mistake: the protesters exposed the whimsical and arbitrary nature of the COVID-19 regime and the moral panic that sustained it. Canadians should welcome this new truth, along with the spectacle of panic the prime minister showed. He had remained hidden in his cottage in fear of Parliament's oversight, but then exposed himself fearlessly among protesters in front of the same buildings he deemed too dangerous for elected members to enter in even fewer numbers than those of the protesters.

In the face of these gatherings, what would we say to the families who were denied the dignity of properly burying their dead loved ones? The government knowingly ordered soldiers to enter virally infected centres in Quebec and Ontario, putting their lives at risk, and then signaled that their comrades were not worthy of public honours. The ungrateful measure of irony was most visible in Nova Scotia. Two fallen Nova Scotia daughters in uniform went without honours, one in the Armed Forces and one in the RCMP. Heidi Stevenson, the Mountie who sought to stop a shooter on a killing spree, gave her life to protect Nova Scotians without distinguishing among racial differences. What do authorities say to their families (and to the families of the Nova Scotia massacre victims who could not be properly grieved for and buried) when Halifax boasted its anti-police demonstration to have been one of the largest in the province's history?

The reaction to one life unjustly lost far and away trumped the COVID-19 moral panic to save thousands, exposing a callous indifference to life outside the unprincipled "guiding" of the media's lens, all without even recalling Stevenson's sacrifice. These blatant inconsistencies in logic, policy, and the application of law in a modern liberal society serve mostly to undermine confidence in law and its application, along with trust in institutions and those who govern.

In both cases, the COVID-19 lockdown and BLM protests, popular emotions swept governments, eclipsing the rule of law and the institutions designed to protect us against the actions of angry mobs. Quite possibly, the large gatherings of protesters had more to do with people being fed up with the lockdowns and taking time to be outside and to express what seem largely unrelated frustrations. One way or another, there was disregard for liberal democratic principles in the simultaneously zealous enforcement of laws for one set of events and the failure to enforce the law regarding another. The failure of the police to enforce the laws constitutes a different kind of abuse.

The jury is still out on the Swedish achievement. With great respect to the dead and the suffering, it may or may not have protected more lives and saved more jobs than the other experiments. But the Swedish achievement in the face of international panic and internal moral pressures lies in Sweden's preparedness and in remaining fiercely true to its political traditions and democratic institutions. In maintaining its independence of action based on established scientific evidence instead of abstract models driven by fear, Sweden preserved and strengthened the crucial bond of trust between government and its civil community. In time, this aspect of the Swedish example may prove to be its most important achievement of this pandemic.

The government and its officials trusted the Swedish people instead of trying to manage them. Swedes in turn trusted their government and officials to protect them without trying to run their lives and trample their traditions of liberty, without undermining Swedish legal traditions, without instituting intimidating police actions, and without imposing outrageous fines on people already hurting from unemployment. Sweden did it without threatening to deprive citizens of free expression, without curtailing the freedom to earn a living and care for one's loved ones, without the crass settling of scores against regions and industries out of favour with the partisan policy of an ideologically disordered government, without the abusive attempt at grabbing powers well beyond all existing emergency legislation, and without giving individual government officials unchecked power that under less panicked circumstances no one would entrust to the entire legislature, let alone the executive. The Swedish experiment already has demonstrated that a society can deal with threats in moderate ways, and that it does not need to resort to undermining its own foundations in response to such a low-level threat. Maintaining and preserving that trust so vital to healthy liberal democratic institutions is a unique blessing a people can give itself, especially in times of crisis. This is a lesson that has been lost on the Canadian political leadership, to the detriment of us all.

Closing Remarks

The COVID-19 pandemic met all the criteria Stanley Cohen described regarding a moral panic. The threat of SARS-CoV-2 took some time to come into focus among the public chiefly because of Chinese obfuscation that hid and then downplayed the threat. In Canada, the prime minister and the federal minister of Health initially declared that the risks for Canadians were sufficiently low that the government did not need to mobilize resources to deal with it. Only after the WHO declared a pandemic on March 11, 2020 did Canadian authorities emphasize the threat that COVID-19 posed and give it prominent play. The virus then became omnipresent in the news cycles, politicians broadcast daily briefings, and the media incessantly reported numbers of infected cases.

Statistical models were used to heighten the threat level by predicting millions of deaths around the world. The evasiveness of the experts, who nearly to a person filled the role of Cohen's moral entrepreneurs, regarding human-to-human transmission, Taiwan, asymptomatic carriers, the inaccuracies and unreliability of models, their eagerness to take "harsh steps" and unwillingness to debate rather than demonize critics and skeptics, contributed additional evidence of expert complicity in the panic. The reality was that fundamental measurement problems continued to exist and that none of the experts wished to address them. Such criticism as existed came from independent sources outside the corridors of orthodox power-knowledge. As expected, they were pilloried and denounced, not argued with, both by the authorized knowers and by the largely ignorant megaphone-wielding media.

The result was an enhanced moral panic. This is why the prime minister warned Canadians as early as April that "it would be absolutely disastrous for us to open up too early or too quickly and have another wave hit us that could be just as bad as this one and find ourselves in a situation of having to go back into quarantine … I don't think we can talk about reopening things until we are confident that we have exactly the plan on responding to future resurgences in place" (*National Post*, April 17, 2020).

More recently, shortly after Governor General Julie Payette read the speech from the throne, Trudeau announced on television that "it's all too likely we won't be gathering for Thanksgiving, but we still have a shot at Christmas" (*National Post*, September 24, 2020). By late October (National Post, October 28, 2020) he was threatening to take Christmas away as well. With such high-powered voices intent on frightening Canadians, we should not be astonished to learn that — at least for most Canadians — fear works. An online Leger poll undertaken for the Association for Canadian Studies found that 83 percent of respondents agreed that governments should order citizens to go masked in all indoor public spaces, a 16 percent increase from July. Eighty-seven percent said it was a civic duty; 21 percent said it infringed on their personal liberties (a decline of six percent from July) (*National Post*, September 23, 2020).

From the start, the moral entrepreneurs — the alleged experts — provided contradictory directives and inaccurate information. The instructions were reduced to clichés that the media and politicians repeated: "Flatten the curve, we're all in this together, we've got your back, save lives!" The media faithfully distilled and delivered a contradictory message: we are all doomed and yet we need to follow the health and confinement directives of the "scientists."

One of the unforeseen consequences of overestimating the virus's lethality and the mission creep by health bureaucrats has been pushback by dissenting and genuine experts and scientists and by ordinary citizens who have suffered considerable economic rather than medical hardship. On September 29, 2020, the *National Post* reported that two days earlier, there had been six new deaths from COVID-19. On October 3, the *National Post* published a letter by Katherine Blanchard of Perth, Ontario, who wrote: "According to StatsCan, there are over 750 deaths in Canada every day, from all sources. We are borrowing huge sums of money, with unknown consequences, and we are destroying our quality of life, all to fight an agent that caused six out of 750 deaths on Sunday." Fear works, for most Canadians, we said, but clearly not for all, as Tegnell observed. Perhaps not at all in the long term.

Tegnell led the Swedish response, which provided some useful lessons for Canadians. Evidence from Sweden not only contradicted what Canadian and American authorities have imposed upon North America but also raised some additional political questions. Central to the Swedish "Total Defence" approach was the requirement to maintain a democratic society characterized by the rule of law. The Swedes, that is, tried to anticipate the unintended consequences of a lockdown and in this way succeeded in avoiding many of them. Canadian data on the malign consequences of the lockdown have not persuaded health bureaucrats to rethink the policies that, they acknowledge, cause too many "excess" dead and damaged Canadians, particularly children. Moreover, unlike North American jurisdictions, the Swedish strategy aimed at not having to lock down, reopen, and then re-lock down, in a cycle with no foreseeable end and no rational purpose. That is, the main significance that the Swedish experience provided was to reinforce the common-sense observation that the lockdown strategy was a policy choice. There was nothing inevitable about it. The governments that imposed it are responsible for the consequences, not the pandemic.

Canadian experts are still a problem, notwithstanding their decreasing authority and the growing shrillness of their rhetoric. In August, Tam announced that, in the fall, COVID spikes could overwhelm the health-care system: "It's preparing for — something could happen to this virus, who knows? Something could change ... What if it demonstrated a certain type of acceleration under certain conditions?" In short, "this planning scenario is ... to over-plan," whatever that meant.[310]

On September 23, 2020, Tam declared that Canada was at a "crossroads." Unless Canadians did as she told them "the situation is on track for a big resurgence in a number of provinces" (*National Post*, September 27, 2020). Even though she allowed that younger people were at lower risk than older ones, she then added a curious remark: "People don't exist in age-group cohorts from morning to night. That doesn't happen." What happens, apparently, is the "spread [of the virus] in any group can spill over to affect [infect?] individuals and populations at high risk for severe outcomes (*National Post*, September 23, 2020). If her remarks meant anything, they exhorted us to pay attention to some very bad news about highly remote possibilities.[311]

---

[310] *National Post*, (August 15, 2020); see also David Ljunggren and Kelsey Johnson, "Canada Says New Waves of Coronavirus Could Swamp Healthcare System," *Medscape*, (August 17, 2020).

[311] In the *National Post*, (October 6, 2020), Chris Selley reproduced another unintelligible message from Tam: "This kick at the curve is a bit different. This time, we've got to bend it like Canadians: give it the old double-double by layering

In this context as well, the Swedish experience has something to teach Canadians. The SARS experience two decades ago led to the establishment of the office of the chief public health officer, the position Tam occupies. The office is tasked with national coordination, planning, and executing strategies for public health. The result, however, was to isolate technical and medical expertise from citizens' common sense. The results have been disastrous: on the one hand, political decisions were made on the basis of the alleged expertise of medical technicians; on the other, the chief medical technician, Tam, has ended up tweeting unintelligible nonsense. Whether Canadians were terrified at Tam's gibberish or amused, nothing good could possibly come of it. Medical experts need the advice of common-sense and non-medical individuals. That is one of the lessons learned from Sweden. In Canada, however, the medical experts do not know this and do not know that they do not know. Nor, of course, secure in the ignorance of their power-knowledge, do the experts have any reason to learn what they do not know or even that they do not know.

The "new normal," to use a familiar cliché, is a regime of truth where mathematical models of infection rates are followed by state directives, action plans, emergency measures, government health communiqués, legal or constitutional modifications, rearrangements of powers for enforcers, speeches, and regular television appearances organized as briefings by politicians. Most of this talk has introduced technical language into public discourse previously used only within circles of experts. It was adopted as a common currency, whether in public or in private interactions. This language and expression became quickly accepted as forms of knowledge that referred to an imaginary reality that nevertheless was understood to be authoritative. This is why these medical technicians presumed to advise the rest of us about personal hygiene, race relations, and diplomacy, about social interactions, sexual intercourse, nutritional choices, and our choice of wines, about physical distancing, avoidance of handshakes, social isolation, masking protocols, and curb-side pickups. All these behavioural modifications, if the medical bureaucrats have their way, will be enforced not by the soft powers of exhortation and the persuasion of a panic but by the hard power of cops and other peace officers keen on deploying their

---

PERSONAL RISK ASSESSMENT and PREVENTION PRACTICES and RECONFIGURING and DOWNSIZING our in-person #ContactBubble, as and where possible." Selley admitted "bafflement" at her message.

power (without the bother of even pretended knowledge) over their fellow citizens.

Finally, there are the policies of the Trudeau government and of the governments of the Laurentian provinces to consider. By the fall of 2020, it was clear that they were all designed to enhance and increase Canadians' fear, especially in Ontario and Quebec, by threatening to lock down the two largest provinces in the country. Inevitably, imposing a second lockdown will be accompanied by increased repressive measures against citizens who resist. In this context, the policy response to COVID-19 has led to increased violations of civil rights as citizens can be anticipated to object and dissent. We have seen a prelude already with the illegal border closures and the encouragement of snitch lines.

The September 2020 throne speech implied a future of unlimited spending and the growth of government control not only of the economy but also of what used to be considered citizens' private affairs. For any government that really believed that "we're all in this together," such an outcome was fully predictable. Moreover, even if the Trudeau Liberals don't believe their own words, they can still act on them. The first step, as Terence Corcoran observed, is to flatten the economy (*Financial Post*, March 18, 2020, October 7, 2020). The astonishing level of social spending and the already weak performance of the Canadian economy unquestionably constitute a crisis. But what kind of crisis? What if Canadians see the federal government's policy as evidence of a strategic initiative rather than bumbling incompetence? Of course, the marginalization of Parliament and the courting of the NDP have enabled the Trudeau Liberals to avoid any serious scrutiny for their corrupt practices. For that basic move of political self-defense, COVID-19 provided plausible cover. The effort to marginalize protesters as conspiracy radicals except when they are protesting the bad behaviour of American cops, and to ignore the real problems of elderly Canadians dying alone in LTC facilities has largely worked. That too can be seen as ordinary Liberal politics.

On October 3, 2020 Leslyn Lewis offered another interpretation of how the Liberals have responded to the opportunities afforded by COVID-19. "What we have been witnessing in Canada is a socialist coup that we, the taxpayers, are funding" (*National Post*, October 3, 2020). She pointed out how Canada is embarked on a perpetual debt scheme, how non-health related issues such as a "green recovery" have become central to the Liberal agenda. Government secrecy has increased as has closer regulation of places of worship and family gatherings. Worst of all, Lewis interpreted the support for able-bodied individuals who are perfectly capable of holding down a job as a deliberate effort "to control our lives through economic dependency." All this stealthy socialism, she said, is "insidious."

Whether one calls this agenda twenty-first century socialism may be a matter of taste. It seems to us to promise all the authoritarianism of a socialist state with the worst aspects of bureaucracy, literally rule by bureaux, by offices. And bureaucratic tyranny, as Hannah Arendt, one of the great thinkers of the twentieth century once remarked, is the worst form of tyranny because it is sufficiently anonymous that it cannot be changed even by the desperate remedy of tyrannicide.

We would like to close this first iteration of our study of the course of the COVID panic with some personal reflections. Kant's arguments can be detected behind the panic and first response by bureaucrats and their nominal political masters. Kant was a first-rate philosopher. He argued persuasively in favour of universalism in the applications of public policies to otherwise quiet populations. His arguments have been orthodox in academic life for over a century. Kant's most famous twentieth-century pupil was, no doubt, John Rawls, whose *A Theory of Justice* has been cited regularly by the Supreme Court of Canada. During the pandemic, Kantian universalism was expressed in the ignoring, for example, of age profiles in the rates people got sick with COVID-19 and died from it. All were to be treated alike, which explains on its own why there was no concern to protect the elderly in LTC facilities or let children stay in school. The universalist policy meant, quite simply, that everybody gets locked down and, for a time, the universalist aspirations of bureaucrats are sated. Arpad Szakolczai did not exaggerate when he described the policy as "madness."[312] Whether this means an end to the triumph of Kantian orthodoxy in political science, which Szakolczai strongly hoped for and ardently desires, is a different matter. Personally, we see no evidence that institutional stupidity is abating.

The docility with which Canadians and even Americans, who are normally less trusting of governments and bureaucrats than are we, accepted the instructions of their betters depended on the internalization

---

[312] See his series of articles in *Voegelin View*, (April 2020).

of the political and ethical teaching of an even more important political thinker, arguably the greatest philosopher ever to write in English, Thomas Hobbes. When Trump returned to the White House after a short stay at Walter Reed Medical Center, he tweeted that Americans should not fear COVID-19 and should not let the disease dominate their lives. He was, of course, sharply criticized, mostly by the mainstream media. No surprise there. He was not, however, the first to attract the wrath of persons, particularly liberals, who seemed to enjoy the experience of fear and demand that everybody must be afraid and show it as well.

In March 2020, R. R. Reno, editor of the Roman Catholic periodical, *First Things*, was similarly pilloried for criticizing fear-mongering last spring. Reno was moved to reflect on the words of Gov. Andrew Cuomo of New York, which were practically identical to Trudeau's words: "If everything we do saves just one life, I'll be happy."[313] Cuomo's words (and those of Trudeau) reflect a "disastrous sentimentalism. Everything for the sake of physical life? What about justice, beauty, honour? There are many things more precious than life." There are indeed, and one of them concerned the economy and the dignity that comes from earning a living rather than being compelled to be a pensioner dependent on the whims of the state. A lack of sensitivity to things more important than physical life is what made it so easy for the Trudeau Liberals to use fear to cover up their own corruption and justify the destruction of the Canadian economy (preferentially destroying the economies of Saskatchewan and Alberta). It is also what makes their actions so unforgivable. The sentimentalism of "saving lives" has come to obscure just about every aspect of both factual and rational truth in our public discourse

For the cowering sentimentalists, particularly the medical bureaucrats, it was not enough to wash your hands and wander about masked. One has to show an elevated sense of anxiety as well — this was obvious when the docs started opining on the symbolic aspects of masking. The great teacher of such a person — even if they never had heard of him — was Hobbes. In his autobiography, which he wrote in Latin verse, he said that his mother gave birth to twins, baby Tommy and Fear. At the centre of Hobbes's political philosophy is fear, fear of violent death first of all, but fear of not so violent death as well. Hobbes is seen by scholars on both the left and the right as the father, or perhaps the godfather, of liberalism.

---

[313] R. R. Reno, "Say 'No' to Death's Dominion," *First Things*, (March 23, 2020).

So far as contemporary liberals (or Liberals) are concerned, the kind of person who was not afraid of death, who was moved by feelings and experiences stronger than fear, has to be dealt with before liberalism — including the Kantian version just discussed — can triumph.

As Daniel McCarthy observed, for Hobbes "only the fear of a violent death is truly rational, and the proper response to that fear is what makes our comfortable lives possible."[314] Anyone who thinks differently, or worse, who acts on the basis of motives more compelling than fear is a deviant, worthy only to be condemned and crushed. Moreover, such persons, say the contemporary stepchildren of Hobbes, have brought this upon themselves: they are bad people. They deny we are all in this together. In part, we have written this report to provide its readers with non-Hobbesian and non-Kantian intellectual sources of resistance.

---

[314] Daniel McCarthy, "A Philosophy of Fear — and a Society of Scolds," *Modern Age*, (Spring 2020).

Index

D

E

I

ideological battle, 61
illness, 5, 15, 17, 37, 40, 43, 71, 78, 86, 122
Imperial College Institute of Global Health, 102
intense crime pattern, 39
International Monetary Fund, 45
invasion of Crimea, 63
Ioannidis, John, 31, 39, 40, 41, 116

J

January 2020, 16-18, 21, 24, 42, 70
Johnson, Boris, 28

K

Kenney, Jason, 27, 59
Kusuma School of Biological Sciences, 12,
Kwan, Jenny, 24

L

Lee, John, 2
Levitt, Michael, 41-43
Lingfa, Dr. Wang, 16
lockdown, 18, 24, 28, 30-32, 36, 39, 40-41, 45, 52, 59, 60-61, 66-95, 99-105, 107, 110,
     113-114, 116, 121-124, 131
lowest risk, 36
Lunar New Year, 18

M

Macdonald, Heather, 30
Marshall, Kathryn, 73
mask, 36, 47-52, 84, 110, 114, 116, 118, 121, 128, 130, 133
matter of epidemiology, 14
measures, 15-16, 25, 27-28, 31, 34, 39, 40, 42, 49, 59, 65-69, 73, 76, 81, 84, 95, 114, 119,
     121, 123, 130, 131
mental health issues, 39
methods of randomization, 55
mission creep, 36, 46-47, 61, 80, 93, 128
model, 24, 26-31, 33, 46, 53, 60, 62, 66, 86, 90, 91, 94, 95, 96, 99, 100, 101, 103, 105,
     119, 125, 127, 130
Montagnier, Luc Antoine, 11-12
moral entrepreneur, 3, 24, 31, 33, 34, 57, 61, 127-128
moral panic, 1-4, 21, 23, 33, 56, 59, 61, 66, 80, 81, 86, 116, 123, 124, 127

N

N95 respirator, 47
National Health Commission of China, 16
National Post, 27, 33, 34, 35, 40, 48, 50, 58, 81, 84, 86, 93, 101, 111, 113, 116, 127, 128, 129, 131
New England Journal, 48-49
New Year celebration, 18
New York City, 118, 133
Norwegian Institute of Public Health, 62
Nova Scotia, 71, 107, 124
number of fatalities, 30

O

Ontario, 77-75, 82, 85-86, 89-90, 101, 110, 114, 124, 128, 131
orthodox mainstream media, 57
outbreak, 1, 3, 15-20, 33, 41-42, 46, 64, 87, 90, 93, 98, 102
overestimation of death, 46

P

pandemic, 1, 3-4, 14, 18, 21, 23, 25, 27, 29, 33, 34-35, 40-41, 43-48, 54-55, 58, 60-61, 68-69, 71-72, 77, 92-93, 100-101, 103, 105, 107, 108-114, 118-120, 125, 127, 129, 132
pangolin theory, 12-13
People's Republic of China (PRC), 12, 14-15, 18-22
People's Liberation Army, 6
percent of transmission, 24
perpetual debt scheme, 131
Pradhan, Prashant, 12
Prince Edward Island, 83, 107
private enterprise, 64-65
propter hoc fallacy, 36
psychological consequences, 52

R

racist attitude, 21
random control trial, 54
RaTG13, 8, 11-13
reaction, 2, 33, 43-44, 48-49, 83, 102, 111, 124
regime of truth, 26, 33, 43, 130

Barry Cooper, PhD, FRSC

Barry Cooper is a senior fellow with the Frontier Centre for Public Policy. A fourth generation Albertan, was educated at Shawnigan Lake School, the University of British Columbia and Duke University, where he received his doctorate in 1969. He taught at Bishop's University, McGill, and York University before coming to the University of Calgary in 1981. For the past twenty-five years he has studied western political philosophy, both classical and contemporary. Much of his teaching has focused on Greek political philosophy whereas his publications have been chiefly in the area of contemporary French and German political philosophy. Over the years he has spent considerable time in both countries, teaching and doing research.

Marco Navarro-Génie, PhD

Marco Navarro-Génie received his education at the CEGEP de Saint-Laurent and Concordia University in Montreal, and at the University of Calgary, where he earned his doctorate. He taught at Mount Royal University, Saint Mary's University, the University of Calgary, SAIT and Concordia University between 1993 and 2013. He is a senior fellow with the Frontier Centre for Public Policy and the President of the Haultain Research Institute, a prairie-focused public policy institute. He is the former executive vice president at the Justice Centre for Constitutional Freedoms and a former president of Civitas. He served as the fourth president of the Atlantic Institute for Market Studies based in Halifax, Nova Scotia, and as vice president of research at the Frontier Centre for Public Policy after his time in academe. He is a former board director of the International Centre for Human Rights and Democratic Development. Navarro-Génie writes and comments regularly on local and national media outlets about Alberta and Canadian public policy. His academic work focuses on radical revolutionary movements and cultural and political identity.

Frontier Centre for Public Policy

Founded in 1997, the Frontier Centre for Public Policy is an independent, non-profit research and educational charity more commonly known as a "think tank." Frontier's mission is to explore options for the future by undertaking research and education that supports economic growth and greater opportunities for Canadians with the goal of improving their quality of life for generations to come.

The work at the Centre is supported by generous donations of many friends from across Canada. In order to assure its independence, the Frontier Centre does not accept government funding.

Frontier includes a world-class team of research fellows including academics, retired judges, and former senior policymakers from both the public and private sectors. Over the years, these researchers have partnered with experts from Canada and around the world.

The Centre is dedicated to foundational Canadian values including individual rights, economic freedom, and a strong civil society that maximizes citizens' choices and standard of living within a market-based economy. The Centre is committed to results-based public policy and high-performance governments that better serve the needs of Canadians. The Centre believes that the best government is as close to citizens as possible (subsidiarity) so that it is effective, accountable, flexible, and transparent.

Frontier serves Canadians by improving the level of thinking, research, and policy discussions, and it focuses on many key policy areas, among which are high performance government, education, civil society, healthcare, environment, local government, asset valuation and divestment, equalization reform, and Aboriginal empowerment.

For more information, please visit our website at www.fcpp.org. You're welcome to get involved with Frontier by donating, volunteering, attending events, and subscribing to the newsletter.

Haultain Research Institute

The Haultain Research Institute is a non-profit educational organization dedicated to finding and articulating solutions that address the structural inequities detrimental to landlocked Canadian provinces. The Institute is named after Sir Frederick Haultain (1857 – 1942), who was a Western Canadian lawyer, an elected representative and judge. Haultain was the first Premier of the Northwest Territories and was first elected to the territorial council in 1887 for the riding of Macleod. Opposed by Laurentian élites, Haultain wanted Alberta and Saskatchewan to be one province named "Buffalo" to be governed with full constitutional powers by a non-partisan administration. This idea was not acceptable to the federal government under Wilfrid Laurier. After the 1905 formation of Alberta and Saskatchewan, Haultain represented South Qu'Appelle in the Legislative Assembly of Saskatchewan as a member of the Provincial Rights caucus and served as the leader of the Official Opposition. He led the charge against the federal control of the province's public lands and natural resources.

The Haultain Research Institute is dedicated to attaining more balanced, fair and renewed societies. For more information, please visit our website at www.haultainresearch.org.

Made in the USA
Monee, IL
06 January 2021